WHEN GRACE FOUND ME

Volume One

Kim Lengling

When Grace Found Me
Volume One

Kim Lengling, Lead Author
She-Writes-Words

ISBN: 9781838283810

Book Cover Design: Listening To Your Voice Publishing

Editor: Ruth L. Anderson

Typesetter: Ruth Pearson

Proof-readers: Ruth L. Anderson and Kim Lengling

Contents

Foreword...i

Introduction 1

1.Finding Faith 7

Kim Lengling

2.Can I Call You Papa?............................ 15

Ruth Pearson

3.Faithful Hands... 23

Nancy Asmus

4.A Silk Purse and Sow's Ear...................... 33

Linda Bookamer

5.I Am More Than A Conqueror 41

Tarnya Coley

6.Grace and Unconditional Love 49

Kathy Gilliland

7.A Christmas Storm 57

Melissa Ginnard

8. When I Met Grace 65

Racheal Graybill

9. It's Time! Forgive Yourself 73

Kimberly Hambrick

10. The Rise of My Undeterred Belief 81

Abbi Head

11. God Was There All Along 91

April Hiles

12. Never Say Never 101

Paula Holabaugh

13. Grace Found Me Patiently Waiting 109

Delphine Kirkland

14. I Needed My Little Girl 117

Cheryl Mattern

15. My State of Grace 127

Arah Perrett

16. Snippets of Grace 137

Sandra Pottorf

17.Thru Grace, Faith. With Faith, Hope.... 145

Rita Preston

18.When Grace Found Me 155

Beverly Smith

19. Fearfully and Wonderfully Made 165

Marcia M. Spence

20. Grace Upon Grace 173

Pamela Vollrath Wheeler

Conclusion 179

Services 181

Foreword

One thing I know about women, they are resilient creatures. And when they come together to solve problems, anything is possible.

But sometimes women keep their battles to themselves. They feel ashamed, avoid others, and don't ask for help. Alone in the world, they hit rock bottom. I've seen this time and again, watching a woman crippled by life's challenges, rebuilding her life using only her deep faith and inner strength. It's only after the recovery process that she discovers that she wasn't alone at all.

Kim Lengling is on a mission to tell stories. Life stories. Empowering stories. Stories of faith, courage, and resilience. A woman of great strength and character herself, Kim looks at others and sees beauty and potential. I think she sees the whole world that way. She knows that life ain't easy, and she's got a few scars to prove it, but Kim also understands the joy of living. And she's spreading hope by sharing these first-hand accounts of grace.

The stories compiled in this book will help you to realize that you are never alone. Your struggles are real, but you can and will overcome them just as the twenty women in the pages that follow have done. And you'll find the joy again. And maybe, just like them, your story and your strength will be the guiding light for others to follow.

I can't wait to see what God has in store for you next.

Beth

Beth Caldwell, resides in Pennsylvania, USA, She is a ten-time author, success coach, the founder of Leadership Academy for Women, and the SHIFT program for women. Her passion is to inspire, empower, and help women succeed in life and business.

Introduction

Have you ever had a vision? One so clear you know it was God giving you a nudge to do something?

I had an experience several months before this book came to fruition. I was sitting on my deck. It was a beautiful summer day. The sun was warm upon my skin with a soft breeze blowing. I sat watching my dog trot around the back yard as chipmunks scurried and birds were busy eating at the feeders that are placed around my yard.

It was a peaceful setting. I felt quiet and calm when an awareness came over me. Colors and sounds became more vivid. Goosebumps popped up all over my body as tears began streaming down my cheeks.

I wasn't sure what was happening. It felt overwhelming yet not in a bad way.

As I sat looking out across my yard, a faint picture seemed to materialise and fill my view. It was as if an old black and white reel movie began to play before me, grainy and jumpy.

In this vision, there was a young lady on her knees with her head in her hands. She was distraught and sobbing. I could physically feel her sorrow and it washed over me in waves.

I began sobbing as I watched her. A memory from years ago came to me. I too had found myself on my

1

knees sobbing and crying out to a God, I wasn't sure I believed in, at the time. I felt those same waves of distress coming from this vision.

As soon as that thought came to mind, a gentle whisper came from behind me. "*There are many who need to accept My grace.*"

It was such a fleeting thing. I was not sure if I had heard a whisper, or if it was myself remembering my own experience.

The vision began to fade and my body began to relax. I realised I had to ask God what He wanted of me. I hesitated, as I wasn't sure what God was asking me to do. I took a deep breath and asked "Father God, what do you want me to do?"

Again, the whisper came "*There are many who need to accept My grace.*"

It came to me as a physical punch to the gut. I lost my breath and whispered, "You want me to write, don't you?"

I received no answer. I leaned forward in my chair, elbows on my knees with my head in my hands when a very clear message came to me. "*God is on the move.*"

The words came to me over and over again, and each time they became stronger as they landed on my heart.

I questioned God. "Father God, do you want me to write a book? Do you want me to ask others to share stories which have scarred them? Oh, Father God! I don't know. I don't know."

The same message was repeated to me. *"God is on the move."*

It was at this moment the book, "When Grace Found Me" was born. Initially, it was only going to be one book, but the response from women, all around the world, was so overwhelming, that it soon turned into the planning of a 3-book series. Indeed, God is on the move.

You are now about to read Volume One and our journey has just begun, with God leading the way.

My prayer as you read is, "May God bless you with His love and grace."

Kim Lengling

Lead Author

When Grace Found Me

Kim Lengling

"But those who hope in the Lord will renew their
strength. They will soar on wings like eagles;
they will run and not grow weary;
will walk and not be faint."

Isaiah 40:31 (NIV)

When Grace Found Me

Chapter 1

Finding Faith

You may be able to lock it away in a room in your mind, but as time goes by and life happens, the door to that room will crack open. As it opens wider, all manner of thoughts and feelings rush at you from every direction.

This may happen at night while you are trying to sleep, or it can happen during the day, sneaking up on you. Your breath becomes shallow and you become hyper-aware of your surroundings.

Rationally, you know that you are okay. You know that you are in a normal setting and as that darkness continues to settle around you and the heaviness weighs down upon your shoulders, it has the power to bring you to your knees.

You fight the weight of the darkness. You do your best to focus. What do you see? What do you hear? What can you touch? You must work so hard to focus.

With hands clenched and muscles tense, you take a deep breath. Do not let anyone see what you are going through. You have become a master at disguising all that is going on within your mind and in your body.

Move forward. Put a smile on your face. There you go, you got through that one. This may happen occasionally, or it can happen daily when you least expect it.

The effort that it takes to keep control is so very tiring at times, and yet sleep is elusive. You know when you fall asleep, dreams will come, and, in those dreams, you will be fighting another battle.

Morning comes. You may have slept for 3 hours. It is the start of another day. Do not look in the mirror. If you look in your own eyes, you will see the tiredness and the sadness that lies within. You feel alone.

There is a storm within you. You often wonder if there is an anchor out there somewhere. A person who does not fear the storm but is willing to chase it. One who is willing to be present. You question your worth. You see yourself as weak. You cry out to God. You believe. But does He hear? Pray.

The storm settles. You have done it; you have made it through another day.

No one chooses to have PTSD. It alters your life and how you view the world, becoming a part of you and you of it. An invisible scar. It is exhausting, and yet, each person who lives with PTSD is a warrior fighting battles no one sees. There is tremendous strength in that.

Make no mistake, there is strength in that.

At this time in my life, I have learned to live with the effects of PTSD. There are still bad days, but not as frequent and for that I am thankful.

There was a turning point in my journey and that is when grace found me.

For years I was angry at God. I did not play the 'woe is me' game. That just isn't in my personality, but I certainly didn't like God and had no interest in talking with Him or letting Him know my heart.

The beginning of change came on a day that found me on my knees on my living room floor. Life had been hammering away at me with a death in the family, a friend had passed away and I was going through a divorce, wondering how I would be able to raise my daughter on my own. The weight became too much.

There I was, on my knees sobbing and crying out "Please, God, please". I was crying out to a God I did not like and wasn't sure I believed in. I wanted nothing to do with Him and yet my cry was "Please, God, please." Amid my cries, I heard a whisper. A gentle stirring within my heart that brought words and those words were "...*but those who hope in the Lord will soar on wings like eagles...*"

I recall my tears slowing as I tried to hear this soft voice and thinking *I know there is a Bible somewhere in this house!* I began pulling open drawers and looking in cupboards. I eventually found a Bible and sat down on the living room floor. I was a bit frantic at that point wondering how to find anything. Was there an index? How does anyone find anything in the Bible?

I became frustrated and tossed the Bible on the floor. I could feel my emotions beginning to build and then I felt another nudge. A nudge urging me to pick up the bible.

The Bible lay open before me where I had tossed it. With nothing to lose, I picked up the Bible and read what my eyes first landed on.

Isaiah 40:30 (NIV)

> *"But those who hope in the Lord*
>
> *will renew their strength.*
>
> *They will soar on wings like eagles;*
>
> *they will run and not grow weary,*
>
> *they will walk and not be faint."*

There they were! The words that had, just minutes earlier, floated around me on a whisper. I realised this was probably God giving me a nudge but I didn't know what to do with it.

You see, at that time in my life, I did not attend church, had no interest in attending church nor having any sort of relationship with God.

Imagine my surprise to find myself in my mid-30s, on my knees of my living room floor with a Bible in my hands?

Was this experience an epiphany and everything magically became right with my world? No, but it was the start of a relationship with God and learning what it means to walk as a Christian. It was a beginning.

I found myself attending church. Still not sure about this whole Christian thing. I would walk into church with a chip on my shoulder and leave with the same chip still there but yet found myself returning each Sunday.

The church at that time was being held in the local high school gymnasium as the original 150-year-old church had burned down.

I took my daughter to an Easter Service, and the gymnasium was packed. I remember that morning so clearly, but I do not remember the sermon. Toward the end of the service, the pastor said, "Let's pray."

As he prayed, I remember holding on to my daughter's small hand on one side and a stranger's hand on the other. As the pastor prayed an amazing feeling came over me. Peace itself was wrapping around me. I had goosebumps on my arms, and I realised that I had tears streaming down my face. I turned to my daughter and asked, "Do you feel that?" I then turned to the man seated on my other side and asked, "Do you feel that?" He had the biggest smile on his face and replied, "Praise God!"

When the service concluded, I had such lightness and peace about me. It was amazing! As my daughter and I left the school, we were holding hands, skipping, and singing one of the worship songs that the worship team had sung.

I have not forgotten that day nor that moment. I believe that is a time when Grace came upon me, or at least the first time I was able to recognise it for what it was.

Since that time, I have witnessed and felt God's Grace land upon me over and over.

Is life filled with roses and sunshine every day? No, but there is something every day for which to be thankful. I realise that we are surrounded by God's blessings if we keep our hearts open to Him and just look.

Life can be so very hard. Don't let your heart harden when those tough times come. Keep your heart open so that you can hear when God whispers his word to you. Let the light in.

Ruth Pearson

"Let not mercy and truth forsake you;
Bind them around your neck,
Write them on the tablet of your heart,
And so find favour and high esteem
in the sight of God and man."

Proverbs 3:3-4 (NKJV)

When Grace Found Me

Chapter 2

Can I Call You Papa?

I must have been about the age of 6 or 7 when I saw the figure of a tall man in the backyard of the house next door. He had a hat on his head and smiled when he looked at me. I wondered to myself, "Who is he?"

The answer to this question came when I was 11 years old. A family friend was taking me to the enrolment evening for my new secondary school. As part of the paperwork, the details of my parents had to be filled in on the form. On the form was written the name of my father. He was the tall gentleman I had seen as a 6 or 7-year-old. It stated what occupation he did, and the fact he now lived in London.

I was 16 years old when I received a phone call from this same family friend. He told me that someone wanted to meet me, and I would have to get the bus and come to his home.

Who is this person who wants to meet me?

My heart was beating fast!

What would I say?

What would they look like?

These and many other questions were going through my mind.

I arrived at the front door and rang the bell. The family friend led me into the front room and introduced me to a big, tall man! "Ruth, this is your dad," he said. As I observed him, I saw he had a hat similar to the one I had seen as a six or seven-year-old girl. The connection in my mind was made.

This was the beginning of a new relationship, we had to build. It was very strange at first. I remember my first trip to London from Manchester to spend my first weekend with him. I did not know what to call him, so I would just hold a conversation and not give him a name. This 'no-name' went on for a couple of years until I came to London to study. After my first year at university, I had to wait a few months for my accommodation to become available as a second-year student. I spent a few months living with my dad. This was the longest time we had spent together. It was at this time he became 'dad'. I was able to call him dad. He now had a name!. Over the following years, we got to know each other well, so his untimely death, in August 1998 had a large impact on me.

I know my experience is not unique, as many children do not know who their biological father is, or do not now have a good relationship with him as an adult. This lack of relationship can also impact the image of whom God is in their life. I know if I am being really honest, this was my experience.

In my life, I have had many challenges and often feel like a modern-day Job, who is a character in the Bible. One day, he lost everything valuable to him. Days later, his health was also impacted.

In 2014, I felt as though my life was falling apart – health, occupation, finances. I did not know where to go. I was at home recovering from my worst lupus flare-up, which included spending three weeks in the hospital. The previous year I had been made redundant, after working as a teacher for over twenty five years. Now, instead of getting a full salary pay whilst recovering at home, I found myself having to survive on benefits and my redundancy pay.

I remembered attending a local church service. Normally when I am ill and unable to walk, I stay at home. But I felt compelled to attend this particular week. The sermon was being preached by one of the matriarchs, whom I had known for years. The title of her sermon was 'Whatever He tells you to do, do it!'.

These were the words Jesus' mum told the servants when the wine ran out during a wedding celebration in Cana. In this, His first miracle, He told the servants to fill the large jars with water to the brim, and then to take some out for the guests. As they followed His instructions the water turned into the best wine anyone had drunk at a wedding feast!

At the end of the service, the lady preacher came up to me and spoke comforting and encouraging words. She said, "Go home and tell God how you are feeling with all of the challenges you are going through. If you are feeling angry, tell Him."

Nobody had ever told me I could speak so openly to God – to share my real feelings.

As a child, I had been told to respect my elders, which meant I would not share my inner feelings. If I could not be real with adults, then I thought I could not be real with God.

Do any of these words resonate with you?

I went home and started to think about what she had said. Who was God to me? I realised I knew a lot about Him, which had been shared with me by others, but who was God to me? As I reflected on these questions and thoughts, I became very emotional as I was now able to connect with my inner feelings, in a new and deeper way. It was at this moment Grace found me, although I did not know it at the time.

This was the start of my journey from knowing about God as an image – just as the first memory of my dad, to me having an intimate relationship with Him.

I could also now describe His 'occupation', step two.

He is my Father.

He is my Comforter.

He is my Friend.

He is the One in whom I place my trust.

He is the One who gives me the courage to face challenges.

He is my Provider.

He is the One who holds my hand.

He is my Forgiver.

These were some of the thoughts which came into my mind as I followed through with the task to do what I was told to do. Now you can see why I was in tears.

I still had the third part of the journey to go. The part that would allow our relationship to become more intimate. The one where I would give Him a name.

This came a few months later. I was watching a movie and heard one of the main characters refer to God as 'Papa' or as we would say 'Daddy'.

I thought to myself, "Can I too call you Papa?" Papa was not a word I had used in the past. This for me would be a big leap of faith, but a necessary one. If I could call God Papa, it would show we have an intimate relationship. It would be a time of healing and reconciliation. A time of a new beginning.

I first started to use the word, 'Papa' in my prayer journal. I started writing 'Good morning, Father God' but with time I was able to write, 'Good morning, Papa'.

I went on a journey with my dad, from an image to a name and occupation, to a relationship. As you have read, I went on a similar journey with Father God.

You may be at the image stage. All you may have is a picture of who God is in your mind. You may have a name and know what He does from a distance.

My prayer is you will get to know God for yourself and have a living relationship with Him.

My relationship with my dad took time to build. It did not happen overnight. Your relationship with Father God will take time to build as well. Spending time communicating with God will bring you closer every day.

My prayer for you is one day, you too will be able to call Him, 'Papa', or some other special name! After all, you have always been His much-loved child, His much-loved daughter.

Nancy Asmus

"Each of you should use whatever gift you have received to serve others, as faithful stewards of God's grace in its various forms. If anyone speaks, they should do so as one who speaks the very words of God. If anyone serves, they should do so with the strength God provides, so that in all things God may be praised through Jesus Christ. To Him be the glory and the power forever and ever. Amen."

1 Peter 4:10-11 (NIV)

When Grace Found Me

Chapter 3

Faithful Hands

God gave me long graceful fingers which I have used mightily all my life.

I was known as a child and then as an adult, as someone who was always doing something with her hands. What I didn't know was how the Lord was preparing me for His works.

By profession, I was a schoolteacher and I was passionate about passing on my skills to my 4th-grade students.

When our children were born, God equipped my husband to provide for our family and allowed me to be a stay-at-home mom.

A pivotal moment in my life came one evening when a gospel-singing family called the Victory Express performed at our church. The group was made up of family members including one daughter who used sign language. My eyes were fixated on their hands. It was as if every movement they made was permanently emblazoned on my heart. I immediately decided to teach myself sign language.

At that time our two daughters were school age so I started a children's choir at our church. It was so exciting to not only teach the words to the songs but to accompany them with signing. These small children were like sponges, craving more, and more. I was fulfilling their needs, but something was missing for me.

We had a performance in our church called "The Living Christmas Tree." This was a glorious yearly celebration of many area churches. The singers stood in a structure towering to the top of the peak shaped like a tree. The light and sound system were breathtaking. The first time our Lord spoke to me His words were "I want you to sign the cantata." But I would need to know hundreds, no thousands of Words! 45 minutes of signing! His answer was simple and poignant "I will equip you." For the next several months I prepared my songbook learning every single word. One Sunday I laid the thick notebook on the altar which made a resounding loud sound. Declaring "This can only be done by your power through me."

With great anticipation, I prepared for the 1st of four performances in December. I was confident yet there were times I would think, *what if I am standing there with the lights reflecting off my hands and my mind goes blank*?

The Friday evening of the first performance arrived. I was dressed entirely in black in a ¾ length velvet top and beautiful silk gunmetal pants. I chose my outfit carefully to honor God but also to accentuate the whiteness of my arms to emphasize my signing hands.

I watched from the back of the church as every pew, even the balcony, was filled with people of all ages. The instrumental introduction to the cantata started and I was standing there alone. A prearranged spotlight was positioned directly on my hands. My hands were slightly damp and cool to the touch. In my mind, I was repeating over and over, *Give God the Glory! Give God the Glory!*

I watched as the conductor directed the last few stanzas before the first musical notes would be sung. He prepared the choir to begin this much-awaited performance. Seconds before I raised my arms into their position, my fingers became extremely warm and relaxed. I knew that my hands were anointed and at that very moment, they were dancing the words to the songs. I knew all of the signs. They could be systematically signed, but this was different. There was a flow of rhythmic moves, expressing emotion, and simply taking delight in my Joyful Praise. I was performing for our Lord and Savior. It just so happened several hundred other people were watching. At the end of the performance I signed four simple words, *Give God the Glory*. God's grace was visible at that moment.

From that point forward I looked at my hands as instruments of the Lord. I said, "Use my hands, Lord."

He has used me mightily. I have sewn costumes for Christmas pageants and a large collection of banners that adorn the church. I witnessed how He slowed down the clock to achieve massive amounts of work in a short interval of time. I never questioned or doubted his plans as my heart leaped to serve Him.

The years of signing the cantata moved swiftly along, often incorporating the growing youth group of our church. At other times a small group and yet other times the entire children's choir was involved.

God was laying out the "steps" of His next big plan. I looked at a small retail space to set up a shop and He said, "Now". I had many spaces to choose from, but I was drawn to a particular space right beneath a set of steps. I told the landlord I wanted my shop set up under the steps. He asked me why when I had many grander spaces to choose from. "Aren't you afraid you will hit your head?" I replied, "If I get too full of myself, I will hit my head but God will keep me humble."

I planned to provide home decorative items and custom artwork for customers. I had learned and perfected a sewing technique called applique. It simply means applying smaller pieces of fabric to a larger piece of cloth.

In September 2006, my shop called *Nancy's Under The Steps* was open to the public. I had wonderful plans, my plans. I belonged to a women's organisation that bi-annually decorated a beautiful Victorian Mansion. Our committee chose the law library and entitled our tree "Glory to God". The tree was adorned with dried flowers from altar flowers. We asked 26 local churches to submit a photo of their church building entrance door. My assignment was to visit each church to photograph its stained glass windows. As I drove or walked around town, I was overwhelmed with the peace of the fall days, the crunching of leaves, and just the smell of the season. To photograph the windows, I had to request permission to enter each church. Even though I had driven past these churches for decades, for the first time I was in complete awe of "their doors".

Every detail and texture to complete this tree was added, it was as if every adornment was divinely chosen. The tree was exquisite and very well received and often referred to as a place of reverence. Immediately following this display of trees, I revisited every church and photographed each door entrance. Although my original plan was to photograph the windows, God had a different plan in mind. I proclaimed these doors must be documented, and it was going to be by me. I prayed to God for a name and it was revealed to me "Adoration". I set about appliqueing each door in the order I was directed. When I completed the appliques of over 30 doors, I had a dilemma. Now what?

An organisation called Aglow International held meetings once a month, and they asked if they could use the pictures to pray for the individual churches. I said I was happy to share my "pretty pictures."

God used these doors over the next several years to draw people, including myself, to share their stories of joys and sorrows. I was gradually brought into the fold and my faith was greatly deepened. I came to realise these pictures were going to be mightily used. It was no longer about selling prints or even an original as that had been "my plan."

Then a dear friend of mine, Joanna, shared she had dreamt all of the pictures were in one place and were all to be donated. I said "That is over four years of work! I have to pray about this. If I give all of these originals away, I will have nothing." I later realised I had been coveting this artwork.

At the next Aglow gathering, His plan was clear. I told the group I had to leave and went to my shop a few blocks away to empty my "storeroom". I laid over 30 originals on the altar that morning so they could be housed in one place to pray and lift all the churches knowing we are all the family of God. I felt a sense of peace flood over me with no sense of loss but overwhelming gratitude for all He had allowed me to accomplish.

I relocated my shop to another area in the same town which permitted me to continue God's work through my hands. It was then that I felt His constant presence as I sewed. I wrote and illustrated two children's books and co-authored a third book. I was asked to do tapestries for the Ark Encounter located in Williamstown, Kentucky, and made four prophetic art creations with God's guidance.

I never asked for this gift which I feel is a blessing. I never know what I will be called upon to create, but my answer will always be Yes, Lord! Use my hands.

When Grace Found Me

Linda Bookamer

"I will pour out my Spirit in those days."

Joel 2:29 (NIV)

When Grace Found Me

Chapter 4

A Silk Purse and Sow's Ear

Comfort words. We've all heard of comfort foods, but comfort words? Simple words, simply stated, simplistically applied, is where and how my heart was led to God.

As a young child, sadness seemed to hit often and hard. A young mother, very sick and blinded by disease, knew time with her loved ones was ending. Tears flowed through our home daily as the reality of her leaving two young children came close and then the time arrived.

How and when my dear Gramma came in, I don't think I will ever know. As my father's mother, she had authority. She never used it in the way one would think. Her perceived strength came from something else. Something deep inside of her. It led to her actions, her thoughts, and her drive. I was intrigued and in love. The sadness that had buckled our family just had to leave at the mere glimpse of her. How could this one person have enough authority to chase away what had held us all captive? Simplicity, and words, which all came across to a child as fun.

As adults were healed by the presence of family and the hope given in Christ, a child needs something a bit more active. I knew this incredibly small in stature woman had something up her sleeve when she gleefully announced for all to come to the table, as we are "eating high on the hog". The roast had to be simmered long, as it was "tougher than Luther's boot". Thus began my Gramma's version of grace.

Simple old phrases that one would chalk up to just nonsense, took on a more spiritual presence in her midst. She created a comfortable atmosphere for a child to learn. I would quietly watch her in the moments she felt she was alone, in her worship with God. Amazed at the sacredness, yet comfortable closeness she held in her relationship with our Father. All the while learning that God loves us where He finds us.

Father married again, and so there were new things that had to be worked out within me. But Gramma stayed. I never asked why, but was later told, it was for me. She didn't want to leave. She felt needed here. Boy, was she. "Don't throw the baby out with the bathwater", I was reminded when complaining about my many hardships with my new mom. Don't throw away all the good things that can become of having a new mom, with your troubles. God can make good out of all things. Romans 8:28. And she was right.

I tried to always stay protected from pain. From the hurt of losing something else in my life. I would hold on tightly to some things, while easily letting go of others. I clung to a security blanket and a teddy bear. I held on to them very tightly, and so laughs and teasing came frequently from my peers. Being called a baby came often. Gramma enjoyed reading the wisdom of others and quoted it when needed. "It isn't what they call you, that should bother you, child, it's what you answer to." W. C. Fields was one of her favorites. I learned it was her way to show me how to be capable enough to turn the other cheek.

As a young teenager, I was shown the example of a tolerant absolutist. She had clear cut lines that she lived by. They gave her boundaries to secure what she believed in. This was important to her. But she always practiced patience and tolerance to others, with much love. "Tolerant with others, strict with yourself", was her way of living a life that she felt at peace with. Yet another way of expressing, "Love thy neighbor".

She was always only "Two hoots and a holler away". I was always told to "Hold my taters". Was blessed more than you could "shake a stick at", and the "cat got my tongue" when being questioned as to why I didn't have a good excuse for something done wrong. Was always reminded that "It takes more than a big mouth", to stand up for what you believe is right, "it takes teeth." And "Never look a gift horse in the mouth" was considered a good time to thank God for His world's benevolence.

Life was to be learned in what I saw each day and perceived as good, then confirmed when I became old enough to take God's word and properly uphold it. Reminders of "Life is simpler when you plow around the stump" and "Don't corner something meaner than you are" with the gold standard of "Sometimes, silence is the best answer" kept a way to handle things in life, most simply. When I doubted His plan, "It is as it should be" was always on the tip of her tongue.

In and out through the hardships of life, we went together. Gramma was always there. She upheld her promise to always be available when needed. All the while showing me that our Heavenly Father was her only source to accomplish all that life would hand us. "When running a race girl, pick the horse with the longest legs" taught me to take notice of what's around me and to make wise choices. I was reminded that "If you always ride in the cart, you will never learn the true distance to town." Comfort words. I hear them often in my mind and heart. Biblically sound, common sense enriched and easily applied.

Gramma is now gone but her comforting words and easily-loved demeanor lives on. I watch my children laugh and enjoy hearing stories and sayings told with the same "decoration" as Gramma told, from the heart of my brother. I now know that she was there not solely for my benefit, but his too.

I am sure she would want me to pass on these comfort words to you with much love, and with just as much of the "special trimmings". Remember child, "God loves you, right where He finds you". And never doubt His ability to make something comforting out of the most humorous, grammatical nonsense. He can "Make a silk purse out of a sow's ear."

When Grace Found Me

Tarnya Coley

"For I know the plans I have for you, declares the LORD, plans to prosper you and not to harm you, plans to give you hope and a future".

Jeremiah 29:11 (NIV)

When Grace Found Me

Chapter 5

I Am More Than A Conqueror

God's grace found me just as I am. My life; my journey. Faced with rejection, low self-esteem, adversity, and fear that shattered my confidence. I did not believe in me. I chose to listen to the negative voices and the hurtful things that people would say to me. These damaging words would go over and over in my head. I pressed the repeat button, not sure how to press STOP. For years I didn't know who I was. I assumed the identity that other people gave me. I was walking around as an imposter. My self-esteem was shattered. I had a distorted view of myself. I could not go on like this.

Fear was another enormous stumbling block. I was afraid of failing, and I felt that I was not good enough. I did not want to let people down. I got caught up in the false illusion of fear. I had to remember, "For God hath not given us the spirit of fear, but of power, and of love, and of a sound mind". 2 Timothy 1:7 (NIV).

On my journey, there have been numerous lessons that I have learned. The most valuable lesson is to appreciate life and believe in yourself. Holding onto the positive affirmation Romans 8: 37 (NIV), "No, in all these things we are more than conquerors through him who loved us".

Going through my struggles has enabled me to learn that every decision I make is a result of a choice I had made. I chose to let my struggles cripple me and I felt I was unable to move forward. I chose to listen to those negative voices.

I had to start making positive choices to see different results. I decided to get up from that place which was destroying my mindset. I was feeling a sense of worthlessness and hopelessness. I had to decide, and I chose to rise above my circumstances. "For I know the plans I have for you, declares the LORD, plans to prosper you and not to harm you, plans to give you hope and a future". Jeremiah 29:11 (NIV).

It all had to start with me believing in me. I had to stop the past defining who I was, or who I thought I was. I went on a journey of healing and through that process, I have found my true worth. Life is a beautiful journey. I needed to change my perspective. I had to change the way I viewed situations.

Throughout my life, I have sometimes felt that I wanted to close the door on situations and walk away. Some of my life experiences were too painful, this prevented me from advancing in my life.

I allowed my negative thought patterns to overtake my life and it changed my perception of how I viewed myself. On reflection, YES, there was pain. YES, there was hurt. I had to walk through that door and learn how to deal with the anguish. I had to persevere even when things got burdensome. I failed at times, but I had to pick myself up, dust myself off, and continue the journey. I had two choices. I could either stay in my situation and my comfort zone or learn from my failures and move forward.

I had to start believing that I was beautifully and wonderfully made. Even though I was rejected by my earthly father, my heavenly father loved me. I find peace and joy in knowing that. I am an overcomer, I now walk in my purpose and calling. I am free, free to be me. I had to affirm myself with the scripture, "…how wide and long and high and deep is the love of Christ". Ephesians 3:18 (NIV)

I started to dream big and set goals. I now seek to motivate, empower, and create awareness to reach the full potential in others. I love inspiring others to dream big. It is so important to be proud of who you are. Be real and be yourself. Do not let the negative opinions of others affect you. Be confident in who you are and know your worth. Remember who you are in Christ.

I began to do things that I never thought I would do. I went to university and studied to be a teacher. I have been a lecturer in Health & Social Care for 15 years. I thoroughly enjoyed inspiring my students to pursue their goals. In 2018, I became an author, speaker, and personal development coach. I was pursuing my goals with confidence, knowing that I can do all things through Christ. It is key that you need to work hard and persevere despite what life throws at you. Never give up, quitters never win. You have to persevere and be determined. You must have a 'no matter what' attitude, I will not quit.

I was listening to a message my Pastor, Paul Lloyd, December 31st, 2017, 'Owning your future'. "You are a champion; you must invest in your own outcome that you want to see in your own life". When I heard those words, something resonated with me.

At that moment I thought, why not write your story? So, I tasked myself to write about the obstacles that I have faced and how I have overcome them. I started by writing one page per day. Before I knew it, I built up momentum and I was writing more frequently. I completed my book six weeks later. I have faced many obstacles in my life; rejection, low self-esteem, fear, and shattered confidence, just to name a few. It was key for me to let the reader know how they too can overcome the downturns of life.

I am a firm believer in encouraging others to be the best version of themselves so they can become everything they set out to be. My God-given purpose is to help others to understand the keys to living a pleasant and fulfilled life. Also exhibiting how they can make those small changes so they can have a better quality of life. It is important to believe in yourself because that is where it all starts.

Now I have discovered my calling, I am a woman on a mission. I am a woman of purpose. Having purpose guides and leads you in the right direction. My purpose has helped me to reach my goals. When you are walking in your purpose, there are certain characteristics that I knew I must possess.

I had to be committed to the task that has been set. Being committed shows that you are willing to follow through. It is one of the most influential principles to be a woman of purpose.

Having compassion has enabled me to focus on other people's needs. Jackson once said; "Never look down on someone unless you are helping them up".

When you are a confident woman you can excel and propel yourself into your purpose. You can be a positive example to others. Having confidence can eliminate self-doubt and negative self-talk.

Being consistent has allowed me to build momentum to keep going. This has brought stability in my life and has enabled me to be more grounded. Even when I do not feel like it, I knew I had to be consistent, focus, and take responsibility.

I have moved from a place of fear to a place of freedom. I continually repeat the words, 2 Timothy 1:7 clearly states, "God has not given us a spirit of fear, but of love and of sound mind". Therefore, if you are operating in fear your mindset is clouded. You will make incorrect judgments and your choices will be based on own intellect. "Trust in in the Lord with all your heart, and NOT leaning to my own understanding. In ALL your ways acknowledge Him, and He will direct your path". Proverbs 3:5-6 (NIV)

God will order your steps; you must put your trust and faith in Him. You will experience an abundance of joy when you eradicate the negativity from your life. When negativity creeps upon you and tries to stifle you, speak those positive words of affirmation. Go back to the word of God, there are many promise scriptures in which you can speak out and believe the words that are spoken. Going through challenges will make you stronger. Know that you can face anything, you are more than a conqueror.

Kathy Gilliland

"Consider it pure joy, my brothers and sisters, whenever
you face trials of many kinds, because you know that
the testing of your faith produces perseverance.
Let perseverance finish its work so that you may be
mature and complete, not lacking anything."

James 1:2-4 (NIV)

When Grace Found Me

Chapter 6

Grace and Unconditional Love

I dedicate this story to my granny, Flossie Bell Ludwig, a woman who was the definition of Grace and unconditional love. When I I think of grace and love, without a doubt, she is the first woman who comes to mind. My granny loved everyone, especially her family. She had 12 children, including one set of twins. In her day you didn't go to the hospital for childbirth, the doctor came to you. But the doctor was late arriving for the first twin and she delivered the baby herself. The doctor arrived in time to catch the second one. All but her last three children were born at home.

After her 12th child was born and about 6 months old, her husband left her and sold the house right out from underneath her, and the eight children still at home. They moved into a converted barn for one year while their church and community built a cement blockhouse. I remember that house. My mom, dad, and I lived in it for a short time when I was little. I remember reading the names of each of Granny's children written on the shelves where they had stored their clothes.

When Granny loved you, she loved you unconditionally. Her youngest son gave her the most trouble. He was in trouble all the time, drinking and using drugs. No matter what, Granny would not turn her back on him. She loved him unconditionally without enabling his behavior. He continued this behavior after she died. Just short of his 40th birthday he had a massive heart attack and was in a coma for a while then on to rehab for one year. Once he was able to talk all he wanted to do was pray and talk about Jesus. He said that he had seen heaven and that Jesus said he was not done with him yet. He has never gone back to his old ways. More than 20 years later he still just wants to pray and talk about Jesus.

It did not matter what you did, Granny looked at your heart, and she always loved unconditionally. Without her influence in my life, I would be a completely different person. She was an amazing woman of God. I was 22 when she went to heaven, but knowing she is there gave me great comfort when I suffered a devastating loss.

In September 1984 as she lay dying in her hospital bed, it was her ex-husband Jack she was asking for. The same man that left her alone with 8 children and no home. When Granny loved you, she loved you for life.

There have been other women in my life who have also shown me grace and unconditional love. Next on the list is my amazing mother Carolyn. She was so much like her mother Flossie in many ways and of course, had the same love and admiration for her mom that we all had. My mom is my best friend. I can tell her anything, no matter what.

I will never forget the night I told her that I had sex for the first time. I was scared and embarrassed. My friends said not to tell my mom, that she would throw me out, especially if I became pregnant. In my heart, I knew that would not happen. My mom loved me unconditionally and would understand that I had made a mistake. So, I waited to be sure I was not pregnant, and I called her up to my room. As she sat beside me, I told her what I had done. She calmly said, "You got your period, right?" I told her that I had, and her next response was "Well it will be ok". That was it. No yelling and no judgment. I was relieved and I admit I was a little surprised how calm she was, even though I knew in my heart how much she loved me.

I also want to share with you the love of my mother-in-law, Margaret Gilliland. It was a bit of a rough beginning as many mother and daughter-in-law relationships can be. Over time, Margaret grew to love me unconditionally and showed me a selfless love of her family. She lived to serve her family. She wanted nothing for herself, only to make her family happy and well-fed. My relationship with my mother-in-law was extraordinary. I loved her and miss her very much. When my father-in-law passed away, I stood with her next near his casket and said to her, "Mom, you are my Naomi and I am your Ruth, I will never leave you and I will look after you." Sadly, she died three months later.

I have also had the privilege to have two amazing friends in my life who constantly show grace and unconditional love wherever they go. The first is Rebecca Royal. I first met Rebecca in 2007. I was 45 and she was 32 with two small children, ages 3 and 5. I was a serious grandma wanna-be. We hit it off right away. I fell in love with her children. In the beginning, we were together all the time, she and I even took her kids to Ocean City. When I suggested, "Let's take the kids to the beach", she said, "You want to take MY kids to the beach?" I said, "Of course! Let's do it." We became even closer. She once wrote me a beautiful card, thanking me for my influence in her life and that she considered me a mentor. Wow, I have never been called a mentor before. I love our relationship; I can tell her anything no matter what it is. She does love me unconditionally. Rebecca may look at me as a mentor at times, but she shows me what grace looks like. We haven't stayed as close as we once were, as children grow, life gets busy and there just isn't as much time. We still love each other very much and I know that I can call on her if I need her. I did check to see if it was ok to include her in my story and to share the beautiful card she wrote. Not only did she give her permission but told me she still looks to me at times as a mentor. Ours is a friendship that has and will stand the test of time and distance. Rebecca means the world to me and I am so blessed that she and her husband Kevin, children Kaitlyn and Andrew have been and hopefully will continue to be an important part of my life.

Another woman I want to share with you is my long-time friend Patti Roemer. I met Patti when our boys were in Tiger Cubs together and she was the Den mother. Patti also loves unconditionally and shows exceptional grace to those around her. She is a true servant of the Lord and people. She loves helping people and sharing her love for our Lord whenever she can. When our boys were growing up, they were constantly together with each of them calling both of us "mom" and we called them both sons. I love spending time with Patti, I can completely be me when I am with her and let my silly side out.

Patti owned and operated a gift shop for many years here in our hometown. I loved watching Patti with her customers. She would show everyone such love and care helping them the best she could. So many times she would be talking to me or someone about something they wanted or needed and she would say, "Just a minute please", and off she would go running upstairs or down to the basement to get whatever it was we asked for. I never get enough time with Patti. I often tell her I wish I could clone her so that I could have her with me all the time. If I could have my very own Patti and Rebecca, life would be amazing!

All these women at different times have shown me what grace and unconditional love looks and feels like. But most importantly, I know without a doubt if I needed anyone of them (of course Granny and Margaret if they were here) would do whatever they could to help me. I know that I can call them, bear my soul to them and they will listen, without judgment or criticism of any kind. They show me the love and grace of our Lord and Savior Jesus Christ.

Melissa Ginnard

"The Lord is powerful, yet patient....
He can be seen in storms and in whirlwinds;
clouds are the dust from His feet."

Nahum 1:3 (CEV)

When Grace Found Me

Chapter 7

A Christmas Storm

The longer we are blessed with living, the more storms we will encounter. The weather that can usher in a new season in a vast array and various intensities. The very fiber of our being is stretched in response.

One such storm hit during Christmas time. I was busy at home, preparing for the holidays. I remember the joy of anticipation that lit the eyes of my little children as we decorated our home that year with lights at the gate and an archway of pine boughs to pass under leading up the cobblestone path to the back door. Thick pine garland strands with tiny white lights lined the backyard picket fence. I had weaved grapevines into a heart-shaped wreath, added a giant red velvet bow, and hung it up on the brick chimney along the side of the house. We admired all our hard work in the cold, crisp evening air. After their baths and some hot cocoa, I tucked my children in bed for the night.

After that, I left for a bit of grocery shopping. With my little ones sleeping and their father to keep watch over them, I could peacefully shop. Few people grocery shop at night which to me was always a bonus. I was humming to myself as I meandered down the bread aisle. Looking down at the shelf to select my bread I suddenly heard that still small voice of the Holy Spirit say, "It's time". I knew in my spirit what He meant.

I did not want to think about the impending storm, so I pushed His words aside and continued working down my shopping list. I had things to do so I finished my shopping then headed home.

Later that night, the phone rang, breaking the silence. "Your Mother has the flu," my Dad said as he explained that the family doctor had been out to their farm earlier that afternoon. This flu was more than a common illness because my Mom had cancer. She had been battling cancer for five years. Dad kept a journal with the date and times for her medications. At that time, she was on oral morphine. I called her every day to check on her. Sometimes she would talk to me; other days Dad would just give me a summary of the day. This call was different. I could hear it in Dad's tone. This was going to be too much for her small five-foot frame to take. I made arrangements for my family and set out early the next morning to make the long trek to the farm.

Dad met me at that door. Inside I could see the little Christmas tree he had put up in the bay window. I handed Dad my coat, turned, and walked down the hall to the room where Mom's bed was set up across from the downstairs bathroom. She struggled to smile. "Lissa, I'm so glad you are here", she said. "I'm here, Mom," I replied as I sat down on the side of the bed. She sat up a little and I hugged her.

During days that followed, I visited with her for a few moments at a time when she was feeling strong enough. She tired easily, but with each little nap she took, I quietly set about making the farmhouse I grew up in feel a little more like Christmas.

Dad did a wonderful job of taking care of her, but I was home to help them both, and to give Dad a much-needed rest. I brought the Christmas decorations down from the attic, put a pot roast to cook in the oven, and got busy adorning every room of our old farmhouse. After dinner and her evening nap, Mom appeared in the living room doorway with a strand of gold-beaded garland in her hands while I was decorating the fireplace mantle. Her strength seemed better. She seemed more like her old self again. Handing me the strand she commented on how much she loved Christmas. The evening was peaceful as I visited with them both enjoying our time together along with the Christmas lights and the warmth from the hearth.

That night, Mom retired to her bed but still wanted to visit so I followed her and sat on the bed with her. She was surrounded by an extensive library of Christian books that lined both sides of the room, floor to ceiling. We chatted into the wee hours of the morning. I finally told her I was exhausted and needed to get some sleep. She hugged me and said, "I love you, my baby". I said, "I love you, Mom" as we embraced before I headed up the stairs to my old room.

The next morning, I received a phone call from my husband about the kids. I had to get back to Akron before they got home from school. Mom was sleeping soundly so I did not disturb her. I kissed my Dad goodbye and headed back home.

After my husband got home from work he wanted to take us out to dinner. Something inside of me told me I should not go anywhere so we stayed in. Later that night the phone rang. It was my Mother's best friend, Shirley. Dad had called her over to the farm a few hours earlier. She told me my mother had just passed away. Stunned and instantly physically weak I fell to the floor crying out, "No Jesus, no Jesus, NO!"

In one split-second, the reality of separation came hurling into my world like a tornado. In an instant eternity was ushered to the door of my heart. At that moment, I could feel a tiny glimpse of God's boundless love in Jesus reaching out to me. To do what I could not do for myself. To buy me back with a price no one could pay except He who is Holy, Perfect and Eternal Love.

When the Holy Spirit told me, "It's time," that was His Grace reassuring me. When I got to go home to the farm for those few days that was His Tender Mercy holding me. When I was able to embrace her, to hear her say 'I love you, my baby' that was His Love embracing me, His daughter, to give me the extraordinary gift of goodbye.

"... when this perishable will have put on the imperishable, and this mortal will have put on immortality, then will come about the saying that is written, "Death is swallowed up in victory. O death, where is your victory? O death, where is your sting?" I Corinthians 15:54-55 (NASB)

Prayers of friends lifted me in a very literal sense in the coming weeks. It was during that time I led a close friend to salvation in Jesus Christ. She told me she wanted what I had. I didn't even know what that was except Jesus. I had never lead anyone to salvation before. I was stunned by my friend's response to my loss, but more than that, I was and am grateful for the opportunity to share my faith. To witness her very real steps of passing from death to life!

It took me years to come to grips with losing my mother; to move on in this life without her. I was saved in her arms when I was 17 years old. Her faith in Christ made me the woman I am today. It's the hard things, the storms that rock our world that draw us closer to Him. It's the winds that blow, and the pelting hail of hardship that causes our faith to become real and not just eloquent words on a page.

Without such storms, Lord Jesus, I would not know you as I do. That my life is in your hands and that I am fearfully and wonderfully made. Most importantly, that I was made for such a time as this.

"Therefore, being always of good courage, and knowing that while we are at home in the body we are absent from the Lord— for we walk by faith, not by sight— we are of good courage, I say, and prefer rather to be absent from the body and to be at home with the Lord." 2 Corinthians 5: 6-8 (NASB)

My heart is grateful knowing the separation of death is a temporary circumstance and that the storms, no matter their intensity, are temporary. Oh, what blessed assurance! See you one day soon, Mom! Thank you, Jesus!

Racheal Graybill

"I am the Alpha and the Omega, the Beginning and the End," says the Lord, "who is and who was and who is to come, the Almighty."

Revelation 1:8 (NKJV)

When Grace Found Me

Chapter 8

When I Met Grace

I lived in a small and beautiful farming community in Northeastern Tennessee. The Smoky Mountains were within my view as well as the stunning Douglas Dam a few miles from my home. I lived adjacent to a small country church whose bells rang regularly, my community was safe, and I had an amazing youth pastor. I was in high school and traveled to area churches to sing and perform in worship. I also regularly sang the National Anthem at the beginning of sporting events and performed at Veterans Day and Memorial Day celebrations.

But life was not as it seemed and I found myself empty, broken, and alone.

As I drove home from shopping in the foothills of the beautiful Smoky Mountains, past the sparkling waters of the inviting Douglas Dam, a voice spoke to me. It was a gentle voice, but one that brought goose-bumps to my arms and legs.

"What are you doing?" The voice startled me. It was only me in my car. I reached forward and turned off my loudly thumping music and waited, listening intently.

"What are you doing?" The voice was louder now, so loud that I looked at the passenger seat to see if someone or something was present. I didn't know how to respond. I knew it was a rhetorical question. One that did not require an answer for the sake of the person asking, but was meant to get me thinking and teach me a lesson.

"Is this what you want for your life? You have no friends. Your life is empty. No one trusts you and you don't even trust yourself. What are you doing?"

By all appearances my life as a young adult was amazing. I had a new car that I had purchased off the car lot with cash when I was sixteen years old. A burgundy 1993 Dodge Shadow with dark tinted windows, a sweet looking spoiler, and low profile tires. I added a new sound system that required an amplifier to handle the two 9 inch speakers as well as the subwoofers I placed in the trunk of my little sports car.

I had a $200 per month allowance given to me out of a trust fund that allowed me to have a cell phone at a young age. (This may seem like no big deal to the youth of our day, but in 1995 this was a big deal!) I was also able to pay my car insurance, buy my gas, and purchase items for my family that not many girls at my age were able to. Coming from an economically lower-income home, this became my salvation and my escape.

Appearances are often vague and shallow. We perceive something to be true based on our own experiences. Assumptions are made based on the way a person looks or how well they perform, serve, or act; but God makes no assumptions. He sees the depths of our souls. He knows our thoughts before we formulate them. He knows our present, our past, and our future and He is present in every moment of our lives, whether we acknowledge His presence or not.

I had everyone around me duped into believing that my life was amazing. No one, except the Lord, knew how unpredictable my home life was. Not many understood how deeply troubled I felt. No one knew how much I hated myself, how ugly I thought I was, how much I wanted to die, and how much I longed to be free from this act of performance. As a teenager, I believed all I truly wanted was a stable and secure home life, my extended family around me, and truth permeating every aspect of my relationships. What I couldn't put into words was the deep residing void in my life. I had yet to discover the ultimate filling of my life's void can not be attained in other things or people. I was searching for someone I had heard of but had never seen. I was searching for someone I had experienced, but never really met. I cried out to God...and He sent Grace.

Grace is often used to describe fluidity, something elegant or flowing. We describe the way a woman walks by stating she gracefully moved about the room. We can interpret the movement of material on an outfit by describing its fluidity being touched with an effervescent grace. We stand in nature watching the graceful stirring of tall grasses or a willow tree's branches moving in the wind's breath and we experience an overwhelming sense of gracious beauty that stirs within us deep tranquility, but not all of my encounters with grace have felt poetic. While grace is all the things I spoke of, grace is also filled with truth and power. And in many of my experiences, grace is clothed in strength.

Grace came running to me that day. Her gentle arms open wide to receive all my "stuff." Grace lovingly accepted me as I cast all my failures at her feet. She saw them. She held them and with tender affection she presented them to my Lord God. He saw everything she was holding, and He cried for my losses. She then threw them into a sea of nothingness that swallowed up all of my failures. She threw into that sea my present junk and my past junk, but she also held within her possession stuff I didn't know I would do. All of it was vanquished. With a loving heart and a face full of radiant joy, she extended her hand to me. And when I was able to receive her hand in mine, Grace ushered me to the throne of Jesus. She was the bridge that took me to my Savior.

Who is Grace, you may ask? I have personified grace, making this adjective a person, but Merriam Webster defines grace as *1a. unmerited divine assistance given to humans for their regeneration or sanctification b. a virtue coming from God c. a state of sanctification enjoyed through divine assistance 2a. Approval. Favor b. Archaic: Mercy, Pardon. c. a special favor: privileged. Disposition to or an act or instance of kindness, courtesy, or clemency. e. a temporary exemption, reprieve.*

When I arrived home from my shopping trip I walked to my bedroom, shut my door, and dropped to my knees in surrender. I needed divine assistance. The ultimate fulfillment of my search was met in a person. The filling of the void in my heart and mind was met in God. What I truly needed was the grace of Jesus Christ.

I first met Grace those moments before I fully surrendered my life to Christ, and I meet her again every moment that I fall on my knees in repentance and humility or cry out for help. Grace is powerful and elegant. She is empathetic and kind. She is strong. She moves across my mind and spirit in ways that can't always be seen but is forever felt. Meeting Grace has powerfully affected my life. I am forever changed.

In reflection, I acknowledge my life has been so peppered with His grace that it is hard to isolate a moment. Grace finds me in the gentle whisper of the wind blowing on my face as I enjoy a warm cup of coffee on the back deck of my cabin in Northwestern Pennsylvania. Grace physically touches me in the embrace of my children who are gifts from a loving and eternal Creator. Grace is in the twinkle of my husband's eye as he looks at me with longing affection and I experience emotions of love and belonging. Grace surrounds me. As the old hymn says, "Grace, Grace, God's grace. Grace that will pardon and cleanse within. Grace, Grace, God's grace. Grace is greater than all our sin."

Now I ask you, "Have you met Grace?"

Kimberly Hambrick

"The intention in the human heart is like water far below the surface, but the man of intelligence draws it forth."

Proverbs 20:5 (NASB)

When Grace Found Me

Chapter 9

It's Time! Forgive Yourself

We never know when God will speak to us. I was at a leadership development seminar earlier this year when we were provided time for quiet reflection. I started to walk out of the meeting room to a bench in the hallway when I heard: "It's time, forgive yourself!" As a person of faith, I knew it was God who spoke those words to me, and I instantly started to cry. I knew I was meant to hear this, but why?

God's words stayed with me for the rest of my time at the seminar and travel home. I would hear His voice daily telling me, "It's time, forgive yourself." But for what?

As a mentor of mine says, the meaning of the word forgiveness is the action or process of letting go of anger or resentment. Like most people, I have had many moments where I had to offer forgiveness to others in my life. From earlier hurts growing up where kids were just cruel with teasing, to unkind words from my family, to my divorce. Though difficult at the moment, I was able to let go of my anger or hurt and forgive the offenders. And for the most part, I let them know that I did forgive them.

But not once do I recall God speaking to me to forgive others. Yet He made it loud and clear that it was time to forgive myself. I spent many hours, days, weeks leaning into His word and wondering what I needed to do. The past few years have been the most difficult ones in my life with two gut-kicks delivered in a row: one personal and one professional. Both forced me into unchartered waters, but my faith, sons, and friends kept me afloat.

The personal situation involved my youngest son. God allows us free will. What we do with it has positive or negative consequences. For my son, his decisions and the consequences following were devastating. We entered a world of lawyers and courtrooms, public judging, and extreme hurt and anger. For the first time, I was struggling. I am a take-charge type of person and I could not find a thread to hold on to. But God holds you up when you need it. I realised that I needed to be there for my son in whatever capacity he needed me. I was strong when I needed to be, but when alone, driving in my car, I was an emotional wreck. I have never cried and pleaded with God as much as I did during this time.

We made our way through the trial and his sentence to the youth correctional facility; my son is forever changed, but stronger. When I think about how he handled this devastating situation, I am amazed at how he accepted the responsibility for his actions, served his time, and met all financial responsibilities on his own; how he harbors no ill feelings toward the opinions of others and their hurtful words. His handling of this humbled me when I was angry at what others were saying about him. I knew if he could forgive, I could as well.

Throughout all of this, I was never once ashamed to be his Mother. I knew I was the exact Mother he needed to get through this. But, reflecting on God's words to me, I wondered if I was still holding on to some guilt as his Mother.

Was there anything I could have done to prevent what happened? Where did I fail him? I made time to talk with my son, after hearing God's words, about how I was feeling. My son said this was all on him. Not on me. He thanked me for standing with him, fighting for him, and loving him unconditionally. I was carrying guilt that served no purpose. I sat in prayer with God and I let it go. I forgave myself for carrying around the guilt that was not mine to carry. I now know that I had no part in my son's decision that resulted in the devastating event. And I now know and fully accept there was nothing I could have done to prevent it.

But I still felt I had unfinished business with God's direction to me. Although I was at peace, I had this tug on my heart that I had not fully understood what I needed to forgive myself for. Proverbs 20:5 "The intention in the human heart is like water far below the surface, but the man of intelligence draws it forth" kept running through my mind. I spent much time leaning into this and praying for strength and wisdom to fully understand.

I spent time reviewing the journal entries I made during this period in our lives. Immediately, the grief and raw emotion leaped from the pages. I was reliving this over and over again as if it had just happened. I heard myself asking God "why" over and over again. And there it was, as a person of faith, I was doubting God when I asked why He allowed this to happen.

Throughout this ordeal, from the moment I learned what had happened, I relied on my faith to carry us through. Yet I was a hypocrite in the one thing I truly relied on, my faith. How could I be a person of faith if I questioned God?

This realization brought an overwhelming feeling of peace throughout my entire being. The tug on my heart was gone. I knew exactly what I needed to forgive myself. I forgave myself for being weak in my faith in God when He was carrying us through. Why did He allow this to happen? If my faith were stronger, I would have never wasted any energy on this question. He did not allow it to happen. I know that. I know it was my son's decision that put this in motion. I let go of my guilt for questioning God. And at that moment, I forgave myself.

Forgiveness of others, even when they have done extremely hurtful things, has always been easy for me. The concept of forgiving myself was foreign. As someone who suffered from limiting self-beliefs for most of my life, why would I even consider giving myself grace? But to move forward and heal, we must forgive ourselves. I am blessed I was open to hearing God's words that day and working intentionally to fully understand why He spoke to me.

When Grace Found Me

Abbi Head

Make Me a Channel of Your Peace

"Make me a channel of your peace,

Where there's despair in life, let me bring hope,

Where there is darkness, only light,

And where there's sadness, every joy."

Johann Sebastian von Tempelhoff

When Grace Found Me

Chapter 10

The Rise of My Undeterred Belief

To play the role of the Virgin Mary in the nativity at the local church ought to have felt like an honor. For me, however, the prospect of portraying a woman so holy, as the imperfect and angry child I was at the age of 4, made me feel deeply troubled.

By the time I reached age 10, my spirit was in emotional turmoil. This realisation floored me and impacted my life into adulthood. At one point, I felt outraged that I had prayed for the health of a loved one which seemed to go unanswered.

My resentment left me with guilt that devoured me. Fury delivered soulless decisions, which I made with knee-jerk reactions. I became addicted to my fragmented morals, principles, ethics, and values which were shaken by self-destructive belief patterns. I still believed in something and wanted to find a new path to finding my release.

Pathetically, those last remnants of hope were shattered in my teen years. The resulting bitterness was unbearable for me as an adult. The course I chose continued to destroy everything that I had learned spiritually and I eventually took solace in self-induced enlightenment.

Moving one hundred miles away from home I presented myself at university with an ingrained judgemental and hostile attitude. Blame was my first focus when things went wrong. I had few friends and spent most of my time studying and creating. Taking a course in the arts became a perfect place to hide my flawed personality.

Within two years, I had managed infestations of mice and insects in my shared house; my long-term relationship broke down, both my friends exited our course, and I was alone again. I even survived being burgled. However, the realisation that some locals were trying to groom me into drugs and prostitution sent me over the edge. That was not going to happen to me!

I was trapped in a position that I could not resolve without drastic action. I had to be brave. I decided the only way out was to lose what sanity I had. I gave it a helping hand with a suicidal dose of one of the most accepted gateway drugs. After a telephone call to my parents, my father rushed to my side to take me home. I was then admitted to a local hospital where I spent the next 3 months. I no longer had to pretend that I could cope. At least I could rest now, or so I thought.

While in the hospital, I ripped up every Bible. I did not deserve what happened to me and I wanted to obliterate everything and everyone around me.

Within weeks I was targeted, violated, and left torn. Mentally incapacitated, physically disabled, I was again powerless to protect myself. My tongue was even curled rendering me unable to speak. Compared to my assailant, I was locked into flashbacks of the trauma with excruciating pains in my head. He was walking freely. Isolated in a side room, screaming inside my mind I found something deep inside me. The embers of my beliefs were re-ignited, but I thought I was dead. Here in this lack of reality, I was at one moment in paradise and the next in an abyss. It felt like a powerful judgment day, as to where I belonged in the afterlife. Had I died unknowingly? How do any of us know when we die? I decided to test reality. I stole some tablets and took three. Once again, I was reacting with desperation and rushed to the Accident and Emergency Room. That was my release. When I saw my father for the first time in the crisp white ward, I felt the magic of peace.

The years that followed have been turbulent, but my experiences fuelled those embers of faith. I always had faith, it was just concealed until I could accept myself and my flaws. I am human. Finally, free of the hospital.

Years later I sat in the local park crying. I knew that every remaining shred of the goodness that I could I remember was stripped bare and exhausted. At that moment I was consumed by grief. I begged myself, "Under no circumstances say that you would sell your soul to be well again." That would be the ultimate temptation. I craved a life with no pain: no flashbacks of trauma, no emotional mood swings, no medication, no failure. Just an everyday life without limits. To believe in a soul and a hell, it follows that there must be heaven. That is where I found my strength, no matter what it was called. Coming from a mixed-faith background I took Solomon's choice on my path.

Returning to university, I attended a talk about women curators. One of the panelists spoke about how an artist's ideas formulate like Big Bang theory. Something derives from nothing. A divine inspiration. As a designer, I often wonder where my creativity stems from. Maybe it is my belief? I have, however, met many people with no faith, yet their value system is righteous beyond measure. At one point it helped to see a Chaplain rather than a psychologist or counselor at that time. I remember him saying that he was not there to convert me. I wondered what I would be converted from and to. I began to get clarity through his guidance. When I eventually crumbled emotionally after a cancer scare and missed our appointments, I felt that I had let him down. However, I realised through speaking to this Chaplain that I was still furious, with myself and something unconscious. There was an opportunity to relieve my rage by yelling at the crucifix in the hospital chapel, but what would I say? "Why?" The prospect made me wince.

I was still terrified to pick up a Bible, knowing that I had destroyed them previously. I was hospitalized around Easter time initially, so it was always a trigger for memories in subsequent years. After seeing the Chaplain I decided to go to church to rediscover the meaning of Easter and deflect from my personal associations. It was courageous to go alone. "Peace be with you" I was told as the congregation spread the word. It sounded to me like "Pleased to meet you." I was soon corrected thankfully. On my second visit I proudly announced, "Peace be with you." to find that this time I should have said, "God be with you." That was my last visit.

The prospect of visiting the church filled me with dread, but not more than encountering the Bible. My first tentative steps into reading any sort of Bible was a book which evidences historical facts in an unauthorized fashion. Found at a music festival stall, I thought this book would be a gateway for a logical person like me. It was not long after that I decided to explore further. Reading a Bible did give me hope that I could find inner peace and a recognition of other faiths. It reignited my childhood beliefs. I still find it easier to tell people that I have Post Traumatic Stress Disorder (PTSD) and Bipolar Mood Disorder than that I have faith. I am not ashamed; I am merely aware of the troubles that opposing beliefs can bring. My father always said, "Never discuss sex, religion, or politics."

It has become more acceptable for us all to be more open about our faith today. As a Community Health Worker years ago, I attended an Interfaith Group. My role as Cultural Competency Lead meant representing our recovery house and our charity at the meetings. It was an eclectic mix of faiths asking questions such as "Should we question God?" My cultural lead role was to ensure that the people we supported had their spiritual needs met. Now I needed to meet my own.

At the beginning of the Covid-19 pandemic, I experienced a mixed emotional state. Accepting a worldwide crisis of this stature was almost impossible. I needed to rely on the strength of my faith to keep from being engulfed. It was as if the whole of the world had been sent to our rooms to think about what we had done to the planet. Many of us were institutionalized within months, removed from our loved ones, lacking physical contact, smothered by masks, and living in disbelief and fear. Keyworkers face the harsh truth on the front line for us. I could work from home and rediscovered a new sense of worldwide unity and connection online. Realising that I was not the only one who felt like they did, I did not want to walk alone. I respect myself and what guides me. Through trauma, my core beliefs were revived enough to begin my journey into a more certain future. I will continue to design that future along with my jewellery business, *Amoreantos*, as well as becoming a public speaker. Feeling robust now after suffering such harrowing emotional turmoil can only be described as a remarkable miracle.

April Hiles

"The Lord himself goes before you and will be with
you; He will never leave you nor forsake you.
Do not be afraid; do not be discouraged."

Deuteronomy 31:8 (NIV)

Chapter 11

God Was There All Along

I grew up in a small town in a loving Christian home. If something was going on at church, we were there. When high school graduation came along, I figured since I was an adult, my parents could not make me go anymore. I am not sure why I was such a rebel about it. I began partying and doing things for which I still struggle to forgive myself.

I became pregnant and was so scared when I found out. The boyfriend I had at the time was not someone I wanted to spend the rest of my life with. I knew he was not the type of guy that would be there for me and my baby. Thankfully I have amazing parents that would always be there.

Six months into my pregnancy, I was feeling uncomfortable at work. When I returned home from work, my parents took me to the hospital where I was immediately put on a monitor to watch for contractions, but there were none.

We later found that it was due to me having half of a uterus. Much to everyone's surprise, after a couple of hours of being on the monitor my water broke. I thought I had wet the bed, but the nurse informed me that I was going into labor. I thought she was crazy. I was only twenty-four weeks pregnant. Who gives birth that early?

I gave birth to a beautiful one pound nine-ounce baby girl, Kylee Ann. As soon as she was born, Kylee was placed in an incubator and immediately taken to the NICU. The only thing I saw was her Barbie doll-sized backside. I was in disbelief.

Three weeks later I received a call from the hospital stating that Kylee had developed a serious infection and she needed to be transferred to Children's Hospital in Columbus, Ohio. I cannot describe the fear I had as I frantically drove to the hospital. I was bawling and it felt as if I was driving in circles.

The next several months were a whirlwind. I would leave work and drive over an hour to the hospital to spend time with my precious daughter. I would have rather spent every moment with her but unfortunately, I was the only parent working and carrying health insurance. Thankfully, my grandma lived in Columbus, so I was able to stay with her when I needed to.

After four and a half months, I was preparing to bring my beautiful daughter home. I had even taken CPR and car safety classes that day. As you can imagine, I was extremely excited and relieved that this day had finally come.

At 1:00 am, I received a call from the hospital. I knew that it was bad news when my mom handed me the phone. They informed me that I needed to get to the hospital as soon as possible because Kylee's legs had started to change colors. I was oblivious to what this meant. I had just held my sweet girl earlier that day telling her about all of the wonderful people that loved her and were excited to meet her.

When we arrived at the hospital, I was surprised to see how dark Kylee's legs were. Several hours later, the doctor called a meeting with us to explain how serious things had become. He said that my baby would not make it through the day. I felt like I had been punched in the gut and the air knocked out of me. I was in shock.

Throughout the day, family and friends who had not yet seen Kylee had the chance to hold my sweet little girl. Whenever I left the room to catch my breath or to use the restroom someone would quickly inform me that Kylee's heart rate was dropping. I would run back into the room, and as soon as Kylee was in my arms her heart rate would increase. This only verified to me what I already knew; we had formed an amazing bond.

Later that day the medical staff felt that it was time to let her go. As I spoke to Kylee, she seemed to fight to stay alive. I was not ready to stop fighting but the nurses asked me to stop talking and let her go. This was the hardest thing I have ever done in my life. My entire world changed that day. I cannot begin to describe the excruciating pain of feeling your child's body go lifeless in your arms.

After going through a total life change of what became my normal for almost five months, I felt so lost. The emptiness and loneliness were unbearable. I remember each time I would see a little girl it felt like a knife going into my heart. Over the years I have had people constantly telling me that I needed a little girl. Every time I wanted to yell and say that "I had one but she is gone."

I began going to the bars and drinking at every opportunity. I had no idea of any other way to cope with what I was going through. There were times that I do not remember driving myself home. I realise now that someone was watching over me. I was fortunate I did not kill myself or anyone else.

One night after work I had decided that I was too tired to go to the bar and that I would take a night off of drowning my sorrows with alcohol and dancing the night away. My mother encouraged me to go out that night which was not normal for her to do. For some reason, I listened to her.

One hour before the bar closed, I met eyes with a young man across the dance floor. He approached me and I let him know that I had no interest in men at that time. I had been burned badly. He was persistent and we hit it off.

I went home that night and asked my mom if she believed in love at first sight. She said that she did and that she had prayed for me to meet someone that night. The young man later told me that he had told his friends that he had met the girl he was going to marry. Our friends thought we were crazy. He had just gotten out of a short-lived marriage that resulted in a little girl and I had not properly mourned the loss of my daughter.

We met the night before he had to leave for two weeks of Army drill. With him, I felt something different than I had ever felt before. After five weeks of dating, he asked me to marry him. I instantly said yes! Not long after, we found out that I was pregnant. We married after dating for only three and a half months.

After losing my daughter I had a strong yearning to have another little girl, thinking that this would help fill the void that I was left with.

Within a few years, we had two wonderful boys, Preston and C.J. I finally felt like I had something to push me forward in life, a purpose. I became pregnant again and felt deep in my soul that it was a girl.

The day we were to find out the gender led to more heartache. The ultrasound showed that there was no longer a heartbeat. I was devastated and felt like I could not breathe. To make matters worse I had to have a DNC to have the fetus removed. This resulted in a severe infection and a trip back to the hospital. After that, my husband tearfully asked if we could be done having kids since he and the boys did not want to chance losing me.

Our first seven years of marriage were difficult. I had not taken the time to mourn the loss of my daughter. He had a three-year-old daughter that seemed to make things harder for me at the time. How was it fair that he had his little girl, but I did not have mine? I truly felt that if there was a God, how could he possibly do this to me?

My wonderful husband and I have now been married for twenty-six years. I just recently realised in the last couple of years that God had shown his love to me by bringing my husband into my life.

My husband has loved me through all my faults and pain and has blessed me with two wonderful sons of whom I could not be prouder. My only regret through all of this is that I did not see what God was blessing me with during the times of struggle. I instead thought he was punishing me for some reason.

Please do not waste precious time failing to realise what God puts before you. I now realise that He had never left my side. He was there all along!

Paula Holabaugh

"And we know that in all things God works for the good of those who love Him, who have been called according to His purpose."

Roman 8:28 (NIV)

Chapter 12

Never Say Never

Loss is something that no one wants to experience, yet it is a part of our lives no matter how much we want to avoid it. Nonetheless, when a loss is so painful that you physically hurt from your experience, that's when you understand just how earth-shaking it can be.

Our Christmas engagement was just after a few short months of a cross-continental courtship and we had planned to be married the following summer. Those plans were underway when the phone call came, the conversation I never thought would ever happen and the conversation which changed my world. If the initial devastation wasn't enough, there was a brief reconciliation followed by even more desolation when he told me of his infidelity. The look in his eyes told me everything because it was there in which I could see the numbing, unmerciful pain, and feel the truth of what had happened.

My world shattered into a thousand pieces that day and my broken heart refused to believe that this was happening. If you've been there, then you understand the pain and abandonment I felt. The thoughts which thundered through my mind, "Why?", "What did I do?", "Why was I not enough?" were the questions that haunted me day after day. A loss like this is painful beyond belief, a physical pain that brought me to my knees. On most days I just wished that God would take the pain away. Over and over again my heart was flooded with questions and "Why wasn't I enough?" was the question which wouldn't let me sleep at night, the question I struggled and wrestled with the most. However, the answers never came.

It took time, so much time, more time than I wanted to spend, but one day led to another and then another, and soon by the great grace of God two years had gone by and the reality set in that I would never see him again. It was time to move forward because I knew that I couldn't stay where I was and I knew that I couldn't go back to what we had shared so I had to press on.

As one year after another passed, I always wondered where he was and how he was doing. Those thoughts would continually linger far into the night through dreams which would cause me to wake in tears. The sleepless nights and the lonely restless days were unbearable at times. It would often take days for me to push those thoughts away as they had to be stuffed deep into the cavern of my heart. I was never going to see him again. All the while I knew that everything I wanted to say would never be said so I simply couldn't think about it.

In the fullness of time, I realised that I had to surrender the pain and move on. I don't recall the exact moment, but that day came and each one thereafter brought with it more and more of God's grace to help me get through the loss I had experienced. Letting go is difficult because your heart wants to hold on to every memory.

More than two decades have passed. The passage of time has helped to cut the threads of pain which had been woven into my heart. And yet, at times I wondered "what if?" Regardless, I was left with so many unanswered questions and those sleepless nights when the memories would return. I surrendered the thought of ever having those questions answered.

It was a beautiful summer evening and the last day of the local county fair when I decided to take my daughter and our exchange student to see the sights. When you go to the fair you understand that you're going to see everyone you know, especially on the last night of the fair. The girls and I decided to get ice cream cones and then head over to see a friend who owned a booth at the fair. I approached the booth and remembered that he and his wife had recently sold the booth and he may not be there. I glanced at the side of the building and there he was so I wanted to stop and say hello. We spoke for a few minutes and then he leaned over and said, "Do you know who's standing behind you?" With a look of surprise, I replied, "No, who?" I knew who had purchased the building but I hadn't given it a second thought...was he here? I looked at my friend and with trembling in my voice, I said, "I need to go, now!" We said goodbye and I just wanted to run out of there, but suddenly I heard my name. In that very instant, fear rose from the depths of my heart and I turned to say a quick hello with the hope of immediately walking away because too much time had passed and I was never going to talk with him again. That greeting turned into a brief conversation where I silently told myself not to look into his eyes because it was there that I knew I would see the look that I never wanted to see again. And yet, I couldn't help but look. I noticed that he was different, in contrast to the last time I had seen him all those years ago. I didn't see the pain in his eyes which had troubled me for so long, perhaps because I was looking at a reflection of myself and the work that God had done in me. We spoke only for a few minutes and I left.

Shaking as I walked away, the flood of questions once again crowded my thoughts. However, I had to push them away because the remainder of the night was spent sharing our local fair with our exchange student. It was dark, and the time had come to leave so we decided that with bellies full of fair food and our feet worn out from walking, we would get popcorn to take home and find our way to the car. I also needed water so I walked to the booth where I had seen my old friend, all the while knowing that I didn't want to see him again. I purposefully walked to the window where another friend was working but was quickly crowded out. I moved to the next window and then to the next where he was standing to take my order for a bottle of water. It happened! Nonetheless, I was not going to talk with him because I needed to get home. I turned to ask my daughter if there was anything we needed to see or do before we left. I moved to leave, and there he stood. "May I talk with you?" he asked.

What could I say? I just wanted to leave, but something in my heart told me to stay. We spent a few minutes catching up on the past twenty years and as the conversation began to wane, he looked me in the eye and said, "I'm sorry. I'm sorry for what I did to you, I'm sorry for what happened all those years ago." I was shocked, I stood there in disbelief of what I had just heard and I was sure that the flood of emotion was going to pull me under once again like the waves of grief which pounded my heart all those years ago. Nevertheless, it was at that very moment that God's grace took hold of my heart and erased every tear, every hurt, every question, and all of the pain. I looked him in the eye and said, "Thank you. I forgive you."

The peace I felt at that moment was indescribable and so fulfilling. The last person in the world that I ever thought I would talk to again was just the person I needed to help heal all my scars and show me just what forgiveness means.

My "nevers" are now God's "watch me work!"

Delphine Kirkland

*"But He was pierced for our transgressions,
He was crushed for our iniquities; the punishment
that brought us peace was on Him, and
by His wounds we are healed."*

Isaiah 53:5 (NIV)

Chapter 13

Grace Found Me Patiently Waiting

Grace found me sitting on my bed preparing to ask God for a divine miracle. My parents introduced me to Jesus at an early age and I believed in Him, but as years passed by, I realised I did not know God. Born with asthma, I prayed with my parents for God to heal me. At the age of 19, I had my last asthma attack. I mostly gave my parents the credit for praying for me than myself as they were true prayer warriors.

Grace heard me asking God for divine healing. I told God countless times how I have read about His miracles, but I was not acquainted with Him in that way. I had a skin disease and it was getting worse and I needed a miracle. "I've heard about you, how you open blind eyes, healed the woman with the issue of blood, but I don't know you like that, Lord." On December 16, 1979, I made a vow to the Lord. I told Him I would trust Him, believe in Him, and stand on His word for my healing. I specifically told Him that I would not receive any medical treatments because I wanted to know Him as a healer.

For a year and a half, Grace found me trying to convince my family and friends that God was going to heal me, God is healing me, and by His stripes, I am healed, only to gaze at faces of doubt and unbelief. I could not convince anyone to believe me except for three people. I was hurt, disappointed, and in amazement how these people that attended church with me for years, singing, teaching, and preaching to me that there is nothing too hard for God. God can do anything. God is a miracle worker, and yet they did not believe God could heal me.

What did I learn about those people and myself? I learned that you could attend church for years and yet you still don't know Him. Jesus told Phillip in John 14:9, (NIV) Jesus answered: "Don't you know me, Philip, even after I have been among you such a long time? Anyone who has seen me has seen the Father. How can you say, 'Show us the Father'? That was an eye-opener for me. I attended church from a child to an adult, yet I did not know Him, believe in Him, nor did I have faith in Him. I needed that spiritual awakening and at that moment, I no longer tried convincing people. I realised it was not about their beliefs, but as long as I believed. This was about my faith, my belief, and no one can walk this journey but Jesus with me. So, I told the Lord, it was just you and me, nobody else, just Jesus and me.

Grace found me deeply reading the Bible and praying as my skin began to look like scales on a fish. Was my faith shaken? No, I believed God was going to heal me. My immediate family questioned my faith, I remained unshaken and unmovable. God's word gave me my strength, my weapon, and it encouraged me day by day. I received phone calls and visits from people trying to persuade me to stop my journey, but they found a woman loyal, dedicated and standing firmly on God's word.

Some people thought I was insane and foolish for what they thought of as suffering in vain. Did they not know that the word of God tells us in 2 Timothy 2:12-13, (NIV) "If we endure, we will also reign with him. If we disown him, He will also disown us; if we are faithless, He remains faithful, for He cannot disown himself."

My consolation came from the word of God in 1 Peter 3:14, (NIV) "But even if you should suffer for what is right, you are blessed. "Do not fear their threats; do not be frightened."

Well, that explained why I had joy in the fight as Satan threw his fiery darts at me. "For it has been granted to you on behalf of Christ not only to believe in him but also to suffer for him." Philippians 1:29 (NIV).

I was reminded of the scripture in John 11:42, (NIV) as Jesus prayed to God about the people standing at Lazarus' grave. "I knew that you always hear me, but I said this for the benefit of the people standing here, that they may believe that you sent me." I pondered in my heart that this will happen to the people that doubt my faith in God. God will show them He can heal me.

Grace found me smiling at Satan's rage as I suffered hair loss, a twisted face, with boils and sores covering my entire body. Grace smiled at me as I constantly rebuked the devil and called him a liar. Grace fought for me as Satan tried to plant seeds of doubt, unbelief, pity, bitterness, and uncertainties in my heart and mind. Grace comforted me as my eyesight was getting dimmer day by day and I could barely walk. Grace blessed me with songs and messages of hope and encouragement on my little radio to carry me through.

As the second year of my journey was ending, grace found me asking God what I must do to help my healing process. God started revealing to me my sins and I found myself repenting daily and asking God to wash me, purge me and save me. Day by day, I felt lighter, happier, free, and who the Son sets free is free indeed. "So if the Son sets you free, you will be free indeed." John 8:36. After days and days of repentance, I beseeched Him again, asking Him what else I must do and what else I needed to know. That night, my Heavenly Father spoke to me, saying, "I'm using you, to let people know, I AM a healer." Eureka! I understood what God was telling me. I will tell people that He is a healer after I give them my testimony on how He healed me.

Immediately my hands went up and I praised God. Suddenly, it was like a bolt of faith entered into my heart. I cannot explain it, but God gave me something special that night. A few nights later, I needed that bolt of faith to fight the hands of Satan. Overnight, sores materialised out of nowhere. Satan was angry because his time of torturing and tormenting me was almost over. That bolt of faith God gave me destroyed the fear that Satan had me captive.

Satan was losing his battle and I knew it. Once the devil is revealed, he cannot hide anymore. Night after night, the devil attacked me with more sores. I sat back and started to laugh at him like Elijah laughed and mocked the four hundred and fifty false prophets at Mount Carmel. I Kings 18:27. I told Satan, "Shoot your best shot." He kept attacking me and I asked him if that was the best he could do? Oh, he did not like that. Then I had to get a little Clint Eastwood on him, and told him, "Come on, make my day".

There was joy in the fight. God gave me joy as I was fighting Satan because He had my back and I was not afraid of the terrors by night. Every day I looked forward to the battle and I went in with my battleaxe, crowning the devil's head with the Word of God. I thought about Samson when he killed a thousand men with the jawbone of a donkey. He was a one-man army. I knew my joy was coming in the morning. I did not know exactly which morning, all I knew was that it was coming.

Finally, one morning, I received that joy. As I woke up, I noticed something different about my right wrist. I pulled my wrist back from my face and spotted a small patch of clear skin. I laughed and leaped for joy, screaming, "Come on Jesus, Come on Lord!" Week after week, I saw the skin of newness. I watched the sores diminish, my face twisting back into place, my hair growing back, boils making head and bursting on their own. Divine healing and salvation came to my home, and I've never stopped telling people how grace found me, saved me, healed, and delivered me. What a mighty God I serve.

"Your testimonies are not just for you. They are about others who will walk in your shoes and need to know how to keep walking. Testimonies are to be shared, not stored." ~Delphine Kirkland

Cheryl Mattern

"Trust in the Lord with all your heart and lean not on your own understanding."

Proverbs 3:5 (NKJV)

Chapter 14

I Needed My Little Girl

The first, most profound, and important time in my life when I feel grace found me, is the day that my daughter was returned to me from her biological father.

You see, I married at the young age of 17 years old. I was too young. I had my daughter at the age of 22. I felt that we were grown-up enough by then to become parents. The 1st year and a half were blissful, and I felt truly blessed with our beautiful gift from God. Little did I know my precious bundle of joy was to have a very rough start to her life.

I remember that my water broke in the early hours of a Sunday morning and I thought to myself 'no, this can't be happening today because God wouldn't have me be in 'labor' when He says 'Sunday is a day of rest'! Ha!

Happiness could not continue as we were not living a righteous lifestyle. We both had our share of selfish ways, but I thought that our love was strong, and hoped parenthood would settle us down. My husband was a musician and the party never ended for him. He was immature and irresponsible. He was the 1st born of an only child, and his grandparents had spoiled him immensely. I would say he was born with a silver spoon in his mouth, but they were simple people, living a very simple life, working hard for everything they had. They bought him his first car and our first home. Unfortunately, he never learned how to make a living for his family. He would quit any job he did not like in a month or less. His parents' work ethic had skipped over him.

We did have a plan in place. Her father would keep her, and I would go to Florida to make a new start. To begin a new and happier life, and my daughter coming to me once I was settled. But God's plan and His good grace came into play and I never made it to Florida.

Unbeknownst to me, my ex-husband had different plans. He and his new girlfriend had moved away and taken my daughter with them. No one knew where they were. A family member who worked at the local employment office has noticed that he had filed for benefits, so she was able to get an address for the lawyer to serve paperwork to my ex-husband.

Again, I was not walking the straight and narrow, but God Almighty knew that I needed my daughter back in my life. I was praying for my situation to get better, but I felt I had nobody in my life to turn to. As I said, I did not know at that time that it was God's intervention and I was not yet out of the woods, I had a long row to hoe. I had a lot of guilt to deal with. Having fallen from grace more than once I knew I had a lot to overcome. Receiving counseling at that time was not so easy.

It was a very confusing and difficult time in my life. I was living on a dairy farm and was the companion and caregiver to a wonderful elderly woman. The farmer had lost his wife and this woman, that I cared for, had been her nurse when the farmer's wife was going through cancer. The farmer and his family would take the elderly woman to church with them as she had no family.

They had put a mobile home for her on their large family-run farm.

I lived in a mobile home with her. We were well suited to each other, as she was in a wheelchair and could not walk and I did not have a car at the time. The farmer would take me to get our groceries a few times a month.

Other than going to church with the farmer occasionally I did not leave the farm often. I had been living there for about 5 months when I finally received legal custody of my daughter. The woman I cared for shared a lot of things about her life with me & I am sure she impacted my life in ways I never realised. Unfortunately, she passed away very soon after I got my daughter back.

I did not know that I was going to be awarded custody. The day after Mother's Day that year he showed up at my door with my precious daughter. I was amazed at how easily he had let her go. I was heartbroken and elated at the same time.

I recall holding her with tears flowing from my eyes. I held her close & could smell that familiar smell of her hair. I remember her eyes being so sad looking. I tried to hide my tears from my baby girl. She was only 2 ½ years old and I am sure she was confused. At that time, I had been away from her father for about 18 months. I knew that I would not return to him because he had physically, mentally, and emotionally abused me. I never thought he would hurt our daughter, but now I know mental scars can be even more harmful. You need to know this was the very early 80's and there was little to no help or services available in my small town like there is today.

I admit that the nine months without my daughter was filled with self-destruction. I abused alcohol; I was self-medicating to ease the pain. Depression lead me down a very crooked lonely path. I became homeless for a short time. I finally moved in with a girl that was not a positive influence in my life, I felt lost and had attempted suicide several times. I felt a great burden of guilt over a failed marriage and allowing my ex-husband to take my daughter.

Then I was awarded custody of my daughter and God knows that I needed her just as much as she needed me.

As the years went by and my daughter grew-up, we attended church and she attended Sunday school and summer Bible school. I wanted her to know it was important to have God in her life. I knew that I had issues to deal with and I realised that I needed to become a better parent. It was not easy for me, but I learned so much along the way.

I did try to keep faith that things would work out for the best, but I knew I had to keep working at becoming a better person, resisting temptation, not allowing bad influences into my life. It was difficult, especially since so much of my life had been living 'on the edge' and letting people lead me there.

I later realised that there were a great many good folks whose paths had crossed with mine. Also, some of my extended family that I had ignored in many ways, had been pulling for me, praying for guidance to get me on the right track again. They were all there in the background as I was very slowly, in God's time, becoming the woman of faith that I am today.

As of now, with the fall of 2020 upon us, I know that God has guided me, healed my health issues, and is carrying me through grief with the recent loss of my sister. I have seen many wondrous signs of His love and the way He is working in my life. How He has prepared me for life without my sister and best friend.

I know that grace is not something earned, it is a favor, or gift that God gives us even though we have not been perfect servants. We only need to believe in God and know that we are saved.

I get weary during these times and I pray for patience. At times I even ask God for a sign that He is still working in my life. Vivid in my memory is one evening as the sun was beginning to set and the sky was dark and dreary as if it could start to rain at any moment. Suddenly, within a tiny spot in a pocket of dark clouds on the horizon, the vision of a bright pink angel lit up the clouds. It was there for only a short moment, but I knew it was there for me.

We must look and keep our hearts and minds open to all that God has planned for us, getting us through the darkness to see all the glorious gifts of His love.

I am blessed to be happily married, a grandmother of three, and have a wonderful relationship with my daughter. I know that God's good grace has found me, every single day that I can get out of bed and have my good health. Thank You, Jesus!

Arah Perrett

"The LORD is my shepherd, I shall not be in want.
He makes me lie down in green pastures; He leads
me beside quiet waters. He restores my soul."

Lessons from Psalms 23

Chapter 15

My State of Grace

Have you heard the saying 'Maybe she's born with it?'

That describes me - I believe that I found Grace at birth. It will be with me until I die, and beyond. I have always had an awareness of Grace. A guiding light, a kind of knowing.

Having said that, there are a couple of things that I should explain – I do not – or have not in the past seen myself as a, particularly religious person. I even flirted with atheism for a few years when I was younger. In retrospect, this was a rebellion against growing up in an orthodox household.

My mother was a devout Christian in a fire and brimstone sort of way. As children, my siblings and I were expected to attend three church services every Sunday. You can imagine how that played out on beautiful summer Sundays when all our friends were outside playing. And yet, there are things that I loved about being part of a religious community. Being a member of the choir, we once featured on *Songs of Praise*! To this day, choral music has the power to raise my energy. Trying on my beautiful, white lace communion dress for the first time at the age of twelve was glorious. I had never felt more heavenly. It was a true community; back in those days my family went through some tough times, and the church was there to support us.

Mum went through a Jehovah's Witnesses phase. For a while, two women came to our home every Saturday to run a children's Bible class. They terrified my sister, brother, and me with stories of damnation. Only Jehovah's Witnesses would be saved; everyone not of the faith, however good, were damned to a grisly, hell-bound fate.

I remember their visits often precipitated frightening nightmares. My instincts rebelled against this vengeful God. Quite frankly, I wanted nothing to do with Him.

My twenties reinforced the idea of a harsh God. Mum died when I was 25, followed, shockingly, two years later, by my 23-year-old brother. Meanwhile, the consequences of my father's alcoholism began to catch up with him; signs of early-onset dementia were emerging. As a family, we were being put through our paces.

So, how did my view change? Through nudges, successes, guidance from odd sources, weird coincidences, and miracles.

This is just one of many examples:

Following the death of our mum and Gary, my sister and I went on a quest for meaning, although I do not think we articulated it in that way at the time. We consulted mediums and attended spiritualist churches on and off for years. I never experienced conclusive evidence of an afterlife through that route, (although I have since come to believe that there is one). However, one medium I visited delivered a startling message that stopped me in my tracks. In those days I was a heavy smoker. She said, 'You have cloudy lungs. Some people can smoke until they are 90. You are not one of them.' I accepted the warning and stopped smoking that day.

A visit to my GP confirmed that I had done so at the 11th hour – just in time to have a chance at a decent life expectancy. It was not, however, all good news. I was diagnosed with Chronic Obstructive Pulmonary Disease (COPD), a serious lung condition that is common in smokers. The stern words of that medium saved my life. More on this later.

During the next few years, I did well. My career blossomed and I continued to receive help from that inner guidance that often put me at the right place, at the right time, with the right people. Do not get me wrong. There have been challenging times. However, I have come out of those experiences stronger, more resilient, and usually more successful.

Sometime in the last 15 years, I began to view myself as agnostic, rather than as an atheist. This was a spiritual rather than a religious shift. My exploration of my beliefs took off in 2017 when I came across a book called The Secret. This is not a religious book. It is based on the law of attraction and our ability to make positive changes in our lives through thought. I was entranced by some of the concepts and it triggered a desire to discover who and what I wanted to become.

I developed a regular practice of mediation, reading widely, attending courses, and journaling that I continue to this day. I also tried to apply what I was learning. During that first year, I focused on becoming a more generous, kinder person who took total responsibility for my actions. I was not looking for any external validation; however, it came anyway. Virtually every relationship I had improved dramatically.

Around this time, a miracle happened. My annual COPD check-up came around, and because my own Doctor's surgery was stretched, I was farmed out to a central triage center for that year only. I remember being annoyed about this at the time. I went anyway and was examined in detail by a specialist nurse. At the end of the session, she said something remarkable. 'I do not think you have COPD.' An 8-year diagnosis was turned on its head. COPD is a deeply unpleasant progressive disease. I had been handed a lifeline. I recall walking out of the clinic in a daze. Could this be true?

Further tests have since downgraded my condition to asthma. Was the original diagnosis wrong? Did a year of meditation and positive inner work enable me to heal myself? Was some outside agency involved? I do not know; what I can say is that this happening finally allowed me to accept myself as a believer.

I must admit that there was one relationship that did not prosper because of my metamorphoses. My partner at the time just did not get it. He became very possessive of how I was now using my time. For him, time spent on my inner development was a time that I should be sharing with him.

I had to choose between moving towards whatever it was I was becoming or moving back so that he could feel more comfortable with the Arah that he wanted.

I chose the former.

Once the decision was made to leave, I acted on it right away. We shared a house and I recognized that I would need to be the one to move. Here again, there was one of those weird coincidences. My then-partner and I were keen walkers. There was a village that we visited regularly during those walks – my favorite place in the entire world. On the day that I chose to leave, an advert popped up for a small house to rent in that highly sought after, difficult to move into, village. Another nudge, another sign. That day I contacted the estate agents and I moved in a matter of weeks. Einstein said that coincidences are 'God's way of being anonymous.' He is right.

I spent a wonderful, life-affirming year in that village. Listening to the owls hooting in the evening, Observing a huge star-filled sky at night. Knowing that I was connected, and the universe was on my side.

This has not been a traditional route to finding God. It is, however, the start of a journey where I have finally accepted that I am part of something bigger than I can fully understand. A huge influence on me now is the *Conversations with God* books written by Neale Donald Walsch. One of my favorite passages in these remarkable books talks about how God speaks to us in a million ways.

"But watch. Listen. The words in the next song you hear. The information in the next article you read. The storyline of the next movie you watch. The chance utterance of the next person you meet.

Or the whisper of the next river, the next ocean, the next breeze that caresses your ear – *all these devices* are Mine; all these avenues are open to Me. I will speak to you if you listen. I will come to you if you invite Me. I will show you then that I have *always* been there. *All ways*." Conversations with God Book 1.

How do I now see God?

As an entity with whom I have a direct relationship. A positive influence; a coach, a source of unconditional love. I am never alone.

I know that I was born with Grace and I will die with Grace.

Sandra Pottorf

*"Then you will know the truth, and
the truth will set you free."*

John 8:32 (NIV)

When Grace Found Me

Chapter 16

Snippets of Grace

Several years ago, on Mother's Day, while at church waiting for worship to begin, I was feeling sorry for myself as no one in my family had contacted me to wish me a happy day. Suddenly, a sweet little girl skipped up to me and said "Hi! I was asked to give this to you!" She giggled as she handed me a tiny box, hugged me, and ran off. Inside the box, I discovered a lovely silver cross necklace and was excited as I placed the chain around my neck, thanking God for someone's thoughtfulness. I was humbled by my selfishness.

Not long after receiving that gift, I was called up front one afternoon to help at the registers at the retail store where I have worked for many years. As customers filtered through my line, a young woman and her mother quickly altered the brisk pace I was working with a few powerful words.

"We are buying pajamas for the lady that is giving me a new kidney!" the young lady exclaimed. My chatter was abruptly silenced. Here she was, sharing the most important news in her life at this moment, with me...and for a few seconds, I was dumbstruck (which seldom occurs).

"Are you scared?" I asked, with sudden tears filling my eyes. "Can I pray with you?" We made a quick little huddle - her mother, the young woman, and me with a prayer for her life to be blessed in surgery and for her subsequent healing.

As they turned to go, I felt the "nudge" as only the Holy Spirit can give me. The necklace...the cross with the Lord's Prayer!

"Wait a minute! I have something for you" I said, excitedly. As I took the necklace from my neck and placed it around hers, she held the cross in her hand and examined it closely.

"This was a gift to me when I was sad, and now it is for you. You can read The Lord's Prayer inside any time and when you feel afraid, just call out His name," I told her.

"I will!" she said, as she and I squeezed tightly in a hug.

"Come back and see me when you are all better!" Those were my closing words. In my heart and soul, I was overwhelmed with God's presence as I felt He was blessing all of us right there. As the moment ebbed away, I thanked my King for the opportunity to witness for Him, and my heart was smiling!

One brisk January day over a year later, I was working in a different part of the store. After opening, the power went out briefly which resulted in having to turn customers away until the computers and registers were all restored. Upon restoration of power, my line of customers was congested for quite a while. As the long line shortened, a young woman who had been waiting patiently in the long line approached my counter, calling me by name. I was startled for a few seconds until I realised it had to be Tiffany, my young friend that was expecting a kidney transplant so long ago! I thrust open the swinging door near me and hurried out to greet her with a hug. We were both emotional. Her mother shared that Tiffany had been anticipating the day that she could come back to the store and show me how well she was doing with her new kidney.

Somewhere in the flurry of emotion and words, I noticed that she was still wearing the necklace. "Oh! It looks like this cross necklace and you have been through some rough battles!" It was discolored on one side and no longer shiny silver. She nodded in agreement.

After we said our teary goodbyes and they left the area, I proceeded to wait on the next lady that had been watching it all. She commented that I looked sad. I wiped my eyes and resumed the rest of my shift. Just as I experienced His presence at our first meeting, my heart was praising the Lord for His grace again, at that moment, as He allowed me to be part of the gift of witnessing this brave young one have a chance at a new life. Grace found even in a checkout line!

Another time at work, I noticed a customer that had been wandering through my area for quite a while. She approached me timidly, "Excuse me, can you tell me if you sell white boxer shorts here? I'm not even sure what they look like!" We went around the corner where some boxer shorts were displayed. I pointed out the white ones, and just like a switch flips a light on, she suddenly started to cry. After a little bit, she wiped her face, and slowly told me. "My husband just died. I am short on money, but I want to give him a good funeral. I was told that if I would buy plain white boxer shorts for him to wear, it would help cut costs. Now I get it - no one will know what he's wearing under that blanket!" We both were giggling and tearful at the same time! She was just muddling through her grief while trying to honor her husband. I was glad that the store had what she was looking for! Her grief stuck with me for a while after that day, like a lump in my throat. Only God could arrange a little humor in an otherwise painful situation.

A few days ago, Mr. L ambled up to my register. I asked for his information and went to find his item. In doing so, I had to kneel on the floor to retrieve it. As I returned to the counter, he asked me, "Did you say one for me while you were down there?" He giggled at his little joke, although his next words were blunt. "You heard about my CT scan?" He paused and looked me right in the eyes as if he expected I would know all about it. "I have lung cancer." I could not seem to form any words of comfort as he left. In some way, I am sure that was God's grace, too.

And then there is Mrs. M... A couple of months ago, she had an urgent request: "I really need you to pray this time," she explained. "My son and his family were on their way here to visit me last week, but halfway here they had to turn around and go back. First, my son, and then his wife and children all came down with a fever! They all have the COVID virus, and my son has it the worst of all. I am so afraid for him. He is in the hospital. Please, please pray for him, for all of them." I had heard about the COVID Virus daily, but this is my first encounter with someone I knew who has family members affected. I needed to adjust my apathetic attitude about COVID after learning about her son and his family. Recently, Mrs. M. was delighted to share with me that her son was breathing on his own, and finally going home!

The people I meet every day in my work are not just part of my job; their needs and concerns are where God intersects our lives, showing us His grace through one another. God loves you, no matter what.

His grace will find you wherever you are -- whenever you least expect it -- and always when you need it most!

Rita Preston

"Here am I. Send me!"

Isaiah 6:8 (KJV)

When Grace Found Me

Chapter 17

Thru Grace, Faith. With Faith, Hope

Grace found me when I was baptized at one month of age in rural Pennsylvania, my parents giving me back to God. Dad was 50 and Mum almost 43; my siblings were teens when my arrival surprised them. Mom surmised God had big plans for me when He blessed them later in life with another baby. They had their share of life and death trials with me as a small child, but God saw to my survival. God had a job for me to do. No parent should bury a child and God spared them that anguish when my illness occurred at the same time my brother was in Vietnam fighting a war and the risk of losing him was just as great.

Grace found me again almost seven years ago when our daughter collapsed near Christmas, just two days before her scheduled induced delivery. I received the call while at my office from our second eldest granddaughter 'Miss Bubbles'. Her exact words still blur, but I will never forget the message: the situation was grave. Our girl and beloved baby were on life support. It all happened so fast. Delivery was scheduled. How could this be happening?

I hung up from the call and asked one of my dearest friends, my boss, to pray. A wise woman of faith, she shared a quote from Padre Pio, "Pray, Hope, and Don't Worry." I relayed that phrase to the grandchildren as best I could. I broke the news to my husband, Robert. I posted on Facebook and asked for prayers, daily. We chose to stay and follow-through on commitments we had for the next few days, as that is what our daughter would want, truly would expect, us to do.

At one function, someone said to me, "If that were MY daughter, I would be on the first plane." Well, this was MY daughter, not theirs, and I knew my daughter. I felt wounded and insulted inside. I would never have said that to someone. Or, have I? What if I were insensitive to someone else's circumstances? I prayed I had not wronged someone that way and that I never would.

I knew when our daughter returned home is when she would need the most help.

There were small signs of improvement for her over the next couple of days, but her baby showed no brain wave activity. We clung to hope.

"Pray, Hope, and Don't Worry."

Another phone call was received on the way to another commitment of the holiday season. "Are you driving, Grandma?" I replied, "Yes." "Call me back when you stop."

We pulled into a parking lot and dialed Miss Bubbles' phone, on speakerphone so that Grandpa was part of the call. Mr. Boyfriend answered, "Hi Grandma, she's on her mom's phone. Hold on." Words we never expected to hear, "Grandma. The doctor says Mama lost brain wave activity."

Tears and sobs. We were numb. Grandpa choked up and Grandpa never chokes up.

The time for disconnection was not yet set. Both our girls were already gone. Their spirits with God. Their bodies remained, battered from emergency measures, worn out, and tired.

Reality changed for us as life ended, was ending, was blurring. There could not be a world without Our Girl.

We entered the event after drying eyes and made our public excuses to leave early. Close friends there knew our prayers and now could tell by our faces what had happened. Hugs and tears were shared.

We followed through the next night with our final commitment of the season, and I am certain we were not the life of the party. We were numb and went through the motions.

We drove to our youngest son's family's new house in Virginia for Christmas as originally promised. They would have understood our broken promise, but Our Girl would have expected us to keep our promises.

We left early from Virginia on the morning of December 26th for our Florida family. Finally, hugs and tears with our loved ones.

When we arrived at their house fifteen hundred miles away, Miss Bubbles stepped out the door to welcome us. Her cheerful nature subdued with grief, she quietly pointed out to us, "You will feel Mom here in the house; she wasn't ready to leave." The older two boys, excited to see us even amidst the past week's sadness, jumped to hug us from behind the kitchen island. Our 3 ½-year-old grandson, the "wee one", was a bit shy, not remembering us well, and having been with his mama when she collapsed.

Minutes passed and Wee One peeked through a doorway. Deep sad eyes met mine. An Angel unseen gently nudged his shoulders visibly. He stepped forward and said, "I love you and you're so beautiful!" I held out my arms and he was wrapped around my neck in a heartbeat; I rocked him, standing there, whispering, "and I love you too, my Beautiful. Always and forever, to the moon and back." He squeezed tighter. With my salty tears spilling over, I finally asked if he would like to hug Grandpa too. Our Wee One with his long locks nodded, staring in my eyes, reaching for Grandpa's strong arms.

Our Girl always exchanged one greeting with me: "I love you, my Beautiful, always and forever." Those were our words, and any close variation thereof, in every text, email, phone call, or in-person greeting.

My heart overflowed nearly to bursting. The warmth of the light glowing around us was invisible, yet unwavering.

Our Girl, our Angel, was holding our baby granddaughter and Christ had his arms around both. God knew our tiny granddaughter in the womb, before her sudden arrival.

I walked into the toy room one evening, attracted by the sound of a droning honeybee. There sat another teen granddaughter (E-E) with a foot propped up and Miss Bubbles' boyfriend hunched over her foot, tattoo wand in hand. A professional tattoo artist, he was engraving a motto on the side of her foot 'With Faith Comes Hope.' E-E looked up at me in pain and asked, "Grandma, is he almost done?" I peeked and he was nowhere close to finished. I shook my head and tried to be reassuring. Grandpa appeared in the doorway and I motioned him over. Ever ready from his combat first-aid training in Vietnam, he took E-E's hand, told her to look in his eyes, and to breathe in and out. In and out. He does not have a single tattoo himself, but he was there for a loving granddaughter who wanted to remember Mama, Baby, and God.

I discovered the three little boys would come to visit with me if I were studying with my laptop for credentials to be completed by December 31st. So, I would disappear to the bedroom, open the laptop, and wait. One of those times, Wee One appeared with his sorrowful eyes. "Gramma, can I draw?" "Sure, Sweetheart." I had plain white printer paper and a purple gel pen, basic office supplies. Poor kid. He started to work. Twisting lips and tongue, he worked. He really tried! Finally, "Gramma, I need help." "What are you drawing, Little One?" "A heart." I drew a purple heart. "Draw more please." I continued to draw until he told me to stop.

Then he showed me, "This is Mama's heart. It broke so she died and went to live with Jesus. These ones are our hearts."

My heart stopped ever so briefly. Catching my breath, "Yes, she did go to live with Jesus. You are so right! And she still loves you just as much and always will!" He nodded, his beautiful soft hair waving in the air. He gave me the drawing with our hearts, drawn by two hands, formed by God, and said, "Please keep this." I have and I will. Grace found us.

Grace has found me repeatedly throughout my life. In my mid-fifties, I am blessed to be touched by the hand of God every day, every night, with every breath I breathe. There has not been a time in my life when I haven't felt His presence with me, near me, enveloping me. When He is distant, it is because I push myself away from Him. He remains there, waiting for me to reach out in my sorrow, in my agony, and joy. He continues to envelop me in His Love.

God's Grace found me early: "Before I formed you in the womb I knew you; before you were born I set you apart; I appointed you as a prophet to the nations." Jeremiah 1:5 (NIV). My parents gave me back to God on the day of my baptism. Our granddaughter and daughter went back to God. The Wee One has no doubt where they went. I have no doubt either.

The very least I can do is answer as Isaiah did when the Lord called to him, "Here am I. Send me!" Isaiah 6:8 (KJV).

When Grace Found Me

Beverly Smith

"For I can do everything through Christ,
who gives me strength."

Philippians 4:13 (NLT)

When Grace Found Me

Chapter 18

When Grace Found Me

My name is Beverly Smith from Manchester, England. I am a pharmacist and I have been practicing pharmacy for 25 years. It was a dream come true for me. However, I realised that I haven't been fully living to fulfill my God-given calling. I believe I am called to encourage, inspire, and to motivate people. Specifically, women who, like me, know it's time for a change.

For as long as I can remember, I have been told too many times that I was not good enough.

Let me take you back to 1981. An excited and hopeful sixteen-year-old Beverly arrives at her new sixth form school.

University was not talked about much at school or home, but I was very bright and a friend of mine who wanted to be a dentist and a teacher from my previous school encouraged me to think about it.

The headteacher at my new school greeted us by saying that no matter how smart we may have been, we were with the cream now. She damaged my confidence and aspirations by humiliatingly insinuating that I was aiming too high to be a doctor.

I wondered if she was racist as she had not treated the white transfers in this way and my other black friend was so unhappy that she left for college. I found that I was not excelling here as I had in my previous high school where I had been Head Girl.

I felt as if there was nobody to talk to about it, but when I told my parents, it caused a massive ruckus because having a job was more of a priority to them. I tried to show them my unhappiness, but I couldn't get through. I was unable to study and one day, I just quit. I remember it felt like a big weight had been lifted off me.

I went to be with my sister in London, where I met a dental student, got a great job in a merchant bank, and was earning so much money that, at 20, I didn't know what to do with it all! Life was amazing and I was having a spending spree as my sister would not accept money from me for rent nor keep.

Eventually, after a misunderstanding, I moved out of her place to stand on my own feet. Initially, I was doing okay, but then the man I was dating broke up with me as he was in the final year and wanted to concentrate on his exams.

Another person making me feel that I was not good enough. It unlocked a feeling of hopelessness.

I decided I was going to take my own life.

Through Divine intervention, however, I was blessed to meet two Christian women separately, within mere weeks of this thought. The first was a lovely lady in my workplace who blessed me with a Bible. It meant so much because I valued the personal inscription on the inside "To Beverly. Study to show yourself a workman approved... rightly dividing the word of truth. 2 Tim 2:15".

The second woman I met while reading a Christian article over her shoulder on the train. We spoke briefly, and she had such little time that she ripped off the corner of her newspaper, wrote on her phone number, and handed it to me before departing the train. But, with my depression and my disheveled room, I forgot about both the Bible and the slip of paper.

One evening, I knelt by my bed, having what many people would consider everything to live for, but feeling hopeless and wanting to end it all. But money, material gain, and the fact that many boys wanted to go out with me didn't feature. I had top exam results and a prestigious well-paid job in the dealing room of a Merchant bank. Money became irrelevant as I could see that being rich by itself didn't make you happy or fulfilled.

Kneeling by my bed, about to take my own life, a thought came into my mind and I went with it. I called out "If there is a God, then you've got to come and stop me doing this and make my life more meaningful. There must be more to life than this!"

I was sobbing. I knew I didn't want to die but I didn't know how to live. I was so exhausted from just trying.

It was at this moment as I knelt, sinking in a flood of tears that I felt a nudge inside me to look up and across the room from where I was kneeling. As I peered through my curtain of tears, I saw what looked like the Bible that had been gifted to me. I was prompted to go over to it and pick it up. God knows that I am right-handed so I put down the weapon that I was going to use to take my life and picked up the Bible. I later found out from Bible study that the Bible is called the Sword of the Spirit, which together with prayer are the most powerful weapons mighty enough for the pulling down of strongholds.

I was again prompted to open it up and as I did so. Through my tears, I saw a line of scripture that seemed to be lit up with a torch. It was from Romans 1:6 which said "And you also are among those who are called to belong to Christ Jesus."

I nearly dropped the Bible. I looked around in my room to see who had highlighted the line for me, but no one was there!

I looked again and read it very slowly, drinking in each word of life.

As I let the words pour into me, it was as if floods of joy rushed in. I was being pulled back up, up to the surface, up from all the layers of bottoms that I had reached. As I was pulled above each new layer of despair, it was as if I heard them snap back shut underneath me. Up and up and up I was being pulled until I was up and out! Free! I was so full of joy, I was bursting, smiling from ear to ear, and yearning to tell someone.

I remembered the lady that I had met on the train - I could tell her! But where in all this mess was that slip of paper? Again, it was like I was following a sat nav with specific coordinates. I picked up one thing then another, shifted a pile of books and something else. There, lying on the floor, was the little piece of paper with her number on it! Within moments of Grace finding me, joy flooded my soul.

I ran downstairs, called the number, and heard this person exclaim "Yay! I've been praying for you!" I was overwhelmed with happiness! "You will never guess what has happened!" I told her. "I'm a Christian too and I want to get to church!"

When Grace Found Me' © Beverly Smith 2020

*When grace found me, the light was dimmed,
I couldn't see*

*Entangled by despair and weighed down deep,
at rock bottom,*

Love stooped down to rescue me,

The arms of grace caressed me,

The kiss of faith embraced me,

As out from the pit of tears,

Almighty God delivered me.

I am free!

When Grace found me, I was given a new, deeper purpose. I went back to college, graduated from university, and I met the man who, 23 years later, is still my loving husband, Philip. We have two beautiful girls: Eleanor-Grace (21) just graduated with first-class honors and Lydia-Faith (16) who just excelled in her GCSEs. Their names testify the truth of Ephesians 2:8, "For by GRACE you have been saved through FAITH, and that not of yourselves, it is the gift of God."

I have since realised that there is still a part of my story missing, so I have written a book about my life entitled *Dare To Dream*. I've begun a personal development coaching business and do motivational speaking so that I can tell all who need to hear my story: "Someone else's estimation of you does not define you or dictate your destination. It's time to step up and let the greatness within you shine."

If I can do it, so can you.

To God Almighty be all the glory,

Selah and Amen!

When Grace Found Me

Marcia M. Spence

"For You formed my inward parts;
You covered me in my mother's womb.
I will praise You, for I am fearfully
and wonderfully made;
Marvelous are Your works,
And that my soul knows very well."

Psalm 139:13,14 (NKJV)

When Grace Found Me

Chapter 19

Fearfully and Wonderfully Made

I was born whole and blessed with an ability to succeed and excel in education, sport, and performing arts. I could do everything I tried, and in most activities, I became adept and skilled. My parents held high hopes for my future, as I did very well in school.

In my teenage years, I fell into some bad habits, smoking and drinking alcohol, I met my first husband when I was 15. After two years together, I just wanted to be with him all of the time. We were in love. I turned 18 in January 1986, and a couple of months later, I asked my stepfather if I could go and live with my boyfriend for a trial period. "Why don't you just go forever?" he replied. I was surprised at his words but got busy packing one suitcase to go and live with my love. Within three months I was pregnant, I was a junior travel clerk in a local travel agency at the time, and I was blamed for the mistakes that another junior had made, no one believed that she made those mistakes. I was the only black employee, and she was a wealthy white girl whose family networked with the directors, I didn't stand a chance. I was at the bottom of the pile, a pregnant, unmarried, and poor teenager. I was fired. I did nothing but accept my lot, I felt a failure.

We were living in a council flat, on benefits, and struggling with debt. We didn't know how to budget. I spent my days and evenings with my' girlfriends' other teen moms. Our children would play in the corner of the room while we smoked cigarettes and talked about our men, our children, and our other friends. I didn't know how to cook, but I tried. We bought chips from the local chippy and shared them with our children. In the evenings, I would push my pushchair home to get my baby to bed and wait for my husband to come home.

Our flat did not have hot running water. Some nights we would hide under the sheets when we heard the mice scurrying across the floor, leaving the baby to fend for himself in his cot. I was living in a world of poverty, provident loans (1000% APR loans), mail-order catalogs, and second-hand furniture. I also bought clothes for my baby boy from a cheap clothes shop called Budget Box. Although it was cheap, it still was a stretch for me, I would put items away on layaway and paid a pound each week until I could take them home. It was a struggle. I had chosen to be an adult, no longer protected at home with my parents and siblings.

I felt that I disappointed my mother, and brought shame to the family, as the life I was living was not what she had hoped for me. Mom fought to get out of the domestic abuse marriage with my father and had high hopes for all her children, but her first who had shown so much promise had fallen off track. I felt depressed about my life too. Being a wife and a mother meant I neglected myself, I let my grooming go, I focussed on my child's and husband's needs, and tried to ensure that we had a decent life. I came from a lovely home, an organized, clean family home. I attempted to emulate this, but I was still a child. Negative thoughts were consuming me. It was dark, and my thoughts were devoid of aspiration. I was sad, and I was lonely, I despaired at the pressure and financial struggle.

One Summer morning, a still small voice said, don't give up. I caught the bus into town with my baby in his chair, I was on a mission to get a job. I browsed the vacancies at the Job Centre and found a part-time receptionist post. I put in my application as soon as I got back to the flat, and the next day I walked to the post box and deposited the envelope.

Three weeks later, I was offered the job, and two weeks after that, I started work. Not long after, probably four months, we were offered a brand new luxury apartment to rent in the town where I worked. The contrast between the two properties was stark. The carpet was a deep pile, and the lounge was three times the size of the front room in the old flat. We also had hot running water and a shower. The gardens were manicured; the complex was set off from the road which was lined with properties with five bedrooms, massive drives, and gardens. It was a posh area. As soon as we turned the corner, we could see and smell affluence. Moving and then living there gave me a feeling of pride. My new environment soothed me and reminded me of who I was and of what I was made of. It was a good feeling. By then, we were expecting another child, and both my husband and I were working, I changed my job, and my new employers paid for me to learn to drive and for my studies. We then bought a brand new car with help from my husband's father, and we had another child, a daughter.

Miracles were happening in my life. I felt a change happening within, I felt more than hope. I was reminded that The Lord had made me in His image and that I *was perfectly and wonderfully made* (Psalm 139:14). I had aspirations, the feeling of failure disappeared, I regained my confidence. I continued to get promotion upon promotion in my career. I took better care of myself, my grooming, and my body. I felt great, secure, and focused, I had a purpose. My career path was found, fulfilling my passion for children until I decided to go to university to gain a degree in Social Work. When I qualified, I found a senior position. By then, my marriage had ended, and I gave birth to a third child, a little girl. I was not married to her father, and we broke up early into the pregnancy. Through the trials of, homelessness, divorce, mental health problems, debt, and chronic illness, each time when my confidence was at a low ebb, I heard a still small voice say, God has not given you a spirit of fear but a spirit of love, power and a sound mind (2 Timothy 1:7). This voice boosted my confidence to push on another day, not by my strength as most of the time I had none, but by the power and might of the Lord my Saviour, to who I am very thankful. When trials come, I hear, Be Still, Be still, and know that I am God. Therefore I put my trust in the Lord as I know that I am not the author of my life, I am not my creator, I am not in control of my destiny. This biblical wisdom has enabled me to overcome and live out my passion and purpose.

I now live on the same street as the first flat mentioned at the beginning of the chapter, in a property I bought when I was in my thirties. The house is located in the same spot as the bus stop where I used to stand with my baby boy in tow. I run my global publishing business from an office in my home. My lifestyle is so removed from the life I lived just 300 meters away 35 years ago.

At the age of 52, I look upon the multitude of situations where I do not know how I came through, and I am filled with gratitude for the awesomeness of God's love and mercy. In this chapter, my reflections are at the beginning of my adult life, a small part of the journey I traveled to become an accomplished professional, semi-retired woman, owning three businesses, a publishing house, an academy, and coaching service for clients worldwide. I have raised three adult children alone. Now I am creating time for me to continue to pursue and fulfill my purpose and to live a joyful, productive life for the remainder of my years. Doing what I love, being who I am, and discovering the world for just me. It is my time now. I plan to live in Portugal with my parents and run my business from my laptop.

God has a plan for our lives. We may take a detour at times, but God brings us back on track, all we have to do is be still and surrender to His will.

Pamela Vollrath Wheeler

"Let us therefore come boldly unto the throne of grace, that we may obtain mercy, and find grace to help in time of need."

Hebrews 4:16 (NKJV)

Chapter 20

Grace Upon Grace

I learned, at a very early age, that God bends His ear to hear us when we go to Him in prayer. From "Now I lay me down to sleep" to "Our Father who art in heaven", my mother taught me my first prayers. But she taught me so much more. She taught me that I could talk to God about all the little and big things that were on my heart. Even before I fully understood the extent of God's grace through salvation, I grew to know that I could lay my troubles at God's feet and leave them there.

Along the way I received answers to prayer for so many things, from the trivial to the urgent. I prayed for God's guidance and leading in my life, even as far as leading me to my future husband. I wanted God to choose that special person with whom I would spend my life. God's grace has led me all along the way.

Over the years I have discovered that God's grace sometimes comes in small, unseen ways and at other times in utterly unbelievable ways that will carry us through the worst times in our lives. God's grace comes to us in times of joy, sadness, uncertainty, pain, illness, loss, grief, widowhood, and in all of life's day to day events. Grace comes when we least expect it, and when we need it most!

Fifteen years ago, with God's grace walking me through, I began a journey that I would most certainly never have chosen. In March of 2005 my beloved husband was diagnosed with Stage IV brain cancer, Glioblastoma Multiforme. I was devastated, to say the least!

So many questions swirled through my mind. How long do we have? What are our options? Surgery, now, to remove the tumor. But, what next? Chemo? Radiation? Would we be able to finish our house? We had been building it, literally from the ground up by ourselves (with occasional help from friends), for several years. It was FAR from being in live-in condition, and our mobile home was on its last legs! How in the world would I manage this without Paul? How could I go on with my life without him by my side?

God's grace covered us both in so many extraordinary ways during Paul's two-year battle against this beast called cancer. These are just a few of the wonderful blessings we were given during this period of time:

- A neurosurgeon who is one of the best in his field

- The tumor was large (6-7 centimeters), but in a very easily accessible spot, and with no spread to other regions of the brain.
- A brand-new chemotherapy treatment that had JUST been released from clinical trials, and would cross the blood-brain barrier.
- That drug, along with targeted radiation to hopefully kill any remaining rogue glial cells, and a second surgery a year later gave us two more precious years together.
- Two years in which Paul was able to go back to work as a reed pipe voicer for a pipe organ builder. The pipes that Paul gave voice to now sing in churches as close as home, and as far away as New York City, the Netherlands, and Seoul, South Korea!
- We were able to take a dream trip to our nation's capital and to Mount Vernon, Luray Caverns, then down Skyline Drive to the Biltmore Estate in Asheville, NC. From there, we drove across North Carolina to see our daughter and son-in-law at Seymour Johnson Airforce Base, then North to a stop in Gettysburg, and across PA to Frank Lloyd Wright's Falling Water house, and back home.

From the time that Paul got home from the hospital, after his initial diagnosis and first surgery, we spent as much time as we had the strength and funds for, working on the house. We were both worried that we would not be able to finish it!

On February 13, 2007 we received the results of Paul's final MRI. The news was what we had hoped not to hear. The cancer had returned with a vengeance, and had spread throughout the brain. Eight days later, on February 21st, I was standing in our unfinished living room when I received a call from Paul's neurosurgeon. He had called to let us know that he had contacted Hospice for us. At that moment we were surrounded by a group of men from our church who had come to look at our house. As I hung up the phone with the doctor, one man spoke. He said, "We are going to finish your house." Four months later, just two months after Paul died, I moved into the house that Paul and I had hoped to share for many more years together.

What a wonderful measure of God's grace was given to us in this loving, unselfish gift of the sacrifice of people's time and energy, in the midst of our sorrow and loss. I know that it gave Paul a great deal of peace to know that I would be able to live out my years in our finished home. After I moved in, I would often tell people "This is the house that love built." It was Paul's and my love that we poured into planning and working on the house, and the love of the people who came to us in our hour of greatest need and finished what we had started and were not able to finish on our own. But, in reality, it was so much more. It was God's love. Above all, it was a confirmation that God's grace abounds in the midst of heartache. It was a manifestation of the promise of provision when you cannot see the way before you, and it was a final gift to put the heart of my dear one at rest.

On April 15th, 2007 my wonderful, godly husband went home to be with our Lord. Paul had been a gifted musician, and I always loved making music with him and using our talents to "make a joyful noise to the Lord". At his funeral I wanted to pay tribute to Paul's love for music and, most importantly, for the Lord. A dear friend played Paul's favorite Chopin piece. Then, at the end of the service, Paul appeared on the screen above the altar, surrounded by a choir. We had recorded a performance of Handel's Messiah that Paul conducted, and I requested that we start the recording at the spot where Paul asked the audience to stand for the Hallelujah Chorus. As the first chords of music began, we all stood to sing the Hallelujah Chorus as Paul conducted us one last time. The Hallelujah Chorus at a funeral? Yes, yes, yes! A thousand times, yes! What more fitting way to pay tribute to a man of God who loved music, and used his gifts to give glory to his Lord and Savior. What more perfect way to acknowledge the Lord by whose grace we are saved, and have assurance of eternal life.

It is so hard, sometimes, to keep walking in faith when all around is dark. But God is WITH us in the darkness; walking behind to give us a push of encouragement, walking beside us to give support when we most need it, and walking ahead of us to clear the way. All along the path He whispers, "I'm right here, beloved. I haven't left you alone in the dark. Keep going. We're almost there. There IS light at the end of the tunnel, and I am in it!"

God's grace. Two little words! Such enormous, life-altering, eternal impact! God's grace is, for the most part, so subtle as not to be seen unless we purposely look for its effects on our day to day life. Its touch is so soft that we don't feel it, and only find its mark later. Grace is God's whispered blessing on our day, His gentle good night kiss at day's end, and His welcoming embrace when we enter eternity.

Conclusion

Did any of the stories you've just finished reading resonate with you?

Throughout this entire journey of bringing Volume One together, the women and their stories touched my heart in ways I was not anticipating. I am positive that one or more of their stories touched your heart as well.

Sharing your personal story and letting yourself be vulnerable takes courage. Sharing your story knowing it will be shared with the world, now that can be intimidating!

The women within this book decided to let that fear go and share their stories, knowing their words had the potential to touch other hearts and also help to promote hope, inspiration, healing, encouragement and so much more.

This journey is just the beginning. Join me as we continue to share our stories of grace, faith, and hope.

Be well, stay well, and be blessed.

Kim Lengling, Lead Author

lenglingauthor@gmail.com

When Grace Found Me

Services

KIM LENGLNG

She-Writes-Words

Making a difference in the world, one story at a time.

Website: www.kimlenglingauthor.com

#kimlenglingauthor

Let Fear Bounce Podcast:

https://anchor.fm/kim-lengling1

LinkedIn:
https://www.linkedin.com/in/kimberlylengling/

Facebook:
https://www.facebook.com/shelikestowritewords

Services

RUTH PEARSON

Preaching

Keynote speaking

Wellbeing coaching and training

Leadership coaching and training

Book writing coaching

Book Publishing

LinkedIn:

https://www.linkedin.com/in/ruthpearsonltyv/

Email: info@ltyvpublishing.co.uk

Made in the USA
Monee, IL
26 January 2021

58485862R00108